Psychoanalytic Diaries of the COVID-19 Pandemic

This intimate book explores the experiences of two psychoanalysts during the COVID-19 pandemic.

It presents Angelo Antonio Moroni's psychoanalytic diary and Pietro Roberto Goisis's clinical diary, two highly personal perspectives that explore the interplay of the personal and the psychoanalytic during a time of collective trauma. Angelo's account, written from his 'camp tent', examines how fundamental, time-tested procedures are suddenly questioned. Roberto's diary is the story of his own experience as a COVID patient, the mutually therapeutic caring relationships he encounters and his efforts to keep his analytical expertise alive and well. The two accounts share painful and graphic experiences of the trauma of the pandemic, and how the authors were forced to reconsider the issues of analytical 'asymmetry' and 'neutrality'.

Psychoanalytic Diaries of the COVID-19 Pandemic will be of great interest to psychoanalysts in practice and in training, and to readers with an interest in clinical and personal accounts of the COVID-19 pandemic.

Pietro Roberto Goisis, MD, is a psychiatrist, psychoanalyst, full member of SPI-IPA and adjunct professor at the Catholic University of Milan, Italy. He has published numerous articles and is the author and editor of four books.

Angelo Antonio Moroni is a psychologist and psychoanalyst based in Italy, and a full member of SPI-IPA. His work includes supervision of Italian and Swiss national health services and collaboration with public and private institutions. He has published several articles and has authored and edited four books.

Psychoanalytic Diaries of the COVID-19 Pandemic

Pietro Roberto Goisis and
Angelo Antonio Moroni

LONDON AND NEW YORK

First published 2022
by Routledge
2 Park Square, Milton Park, Abingdon, Oxon OX14 4RN

and by Routledge
605 Third Avenue, New York, NY 10158

Routledge is an imprint of the Taylor & Francis Group, an informa business

© 2022 Pietro Roberto Goisis and Angelo Antonio Moroni

The rights of Pietro Roberto Goisis and Angelo Antonio Moroni to be identified as authors of this work has been asserted in accordance with sections 77 and 78 of the Copyright, Designs and Patents Act 1988.

All rights reserved. No part of this book may be reprinted or reproduced or utilised in any form or by any electronic, mechanical, or other means, now known or hereafter invented, including photocopying and recording, or in any information storage or retrieval system, without permission in writing from the publishers.

Trademark notice: Product or corporate names may be trademarks or registered trademarks, and are used only for identification and explanation without intent to infringe.

British Library Cataloguing-in-Publication Data
A catalogue record for this book is available from the British Library

Library of Congress Cataloging-in-Publication Data
Names: Goisis, Pietro Roberto, author. | Moroni, Angelo Antonio, author.
Title: Psychoanalytic diaries of the COVID-19 pandemic / Pietro Roberto Goisis and Angelo Antonio Moroni ; translation, Linda B. D'Arrigo, MD, psychiatrist, translator, Pavia, Italy, Robert F. Taylor, Business and Financial Translations, San Diego, USA.
Description: Milton Park, Abingdon, Oxon ; New York, NY : Routledge, 2022. | Includes bibliographical references and index. | Summary: "This intimate book explores the experiences of two psychoanalysts during the COVID-19 pandemic. It presents Angelo Moroni's psychoanalytic diary and Pietro Roberto Goisis's clinical diary, two highly personal perspectives that explore the interplay of the personal and the psychoanalytic during a time of collective trauma. Angelo's account, written from his 'camp tent', examines how fundamental, time-tested procedures are suddenly questioned. Roberto's diary is the story of his own experience as a COVID patient, the mutually therapeutic caring relationships he encounters and his efforts to keep his analytical expertise alive and well. The two accounts share painful and graphic experiences of the trauma of the pandemic, and how the authors were forced to reconsider the issues of analytical 'asymmetry' and 'neutrality'. Psychoanalytic Diaries of the COVID-19 Pandemic will be of great interest to psychoanalysts in practice and in training, and to readers with an interest in clinical and personal accounts of the COVID-19 pandemic"-- Provided by publisher.
Identifiers: LCCN 2021032716 (print) | LCCN 2021032717 (ebook) | ISBN 9781032056906 (hardback) | ISBN 9781032056913 (paperback) | ISBN 9781003198734 (ebook)
Subjects: LCSH: COVID-19 (Disease)--Psychological aspects. | COVID-19 (Disease)--Diaries. | Psychotherapy. | Psychoanalysts--Italy--Biography.
Classification: LCC RA644.C67 G644 2022 (print) | LCC RA644.C67 (ebook) | DDC 616.2/4140019--dc23
LC record available at https://lccn.loc.gov/2021032716
LC ebook record available at https://lccn.loc.gov/2021032717

ISBN: 978-1-032-05690-6 (hbk)
ISBN: 978-1-032-05691-3 (pbk)
ISBN: 978-1-003-19873-4 (ebk)

DOI: 10.4324/9781003198734

Typeset in Times New Roman
by Taylor & Francis Books

Translation
Linda B. D'Arrigo, MD, psychiatrist, translator, Pavia, Italy
Robert F. Taylor, Business and Financial Translations, San Diego, USA

To Cristina

To Lucia

Contents

	Acknowledgements	viii
	Introduction	1
1	Psychoanalytic diary in the lockdown ANGELO ANTONIO MORONI	5
2	Clinical diary of a psychoanalyst in the disease PIETRO ROBERTO GOISIS	68
	Conclusions	93
	Bibliography	96
	Filmography	97
	Index	100

Acknowledgements

Angelo Antonio Moroni

My first heartfelt thanks go to all the patients who have helped me face this truly complex phase of my professional career by adapting to new types of heretofore-untested settings used for psychoanalysis in such a sudden and intense way, and by wanting, nonetheless, to continue the analysis they started with me.

A special thought goes to all my patients who are doctors, and who, via Skype, brought me with them to Covid-19 wards, where they worked hard for months to safeguard all of us, saved lives, accompanied many patients at the end of their journey, and still took time to share their pain with me.

I would also like to say a special thanks to Tiberia de Matteis, a theatre critic for the newspaper *Il Tempo*, for her invaluable suggestions, thoughtful sensitivity and essential assistance in the final editing of this diary.

Thanks also to the many colleagues and friends who have read and commented on the day-to-day diary on my Facebook page.

My most heartfelt gratitude goes to Roberto Goisis, who so intimately shared the experience of his illness with me, for the authentic emotions that he was able to convey to me in the darkest days of the epidemic.

Pietro Roberto Goisis

First of all, I would like to thank those who "saved" me. It is a long, unending list.

At the top of the list are the healthcare staff that I met at the first critical moment. Everyone played a fundamental role and occupies a special place in my heart and in the memory of what happened to me. These include Viviana Gallorini, Roberto Elli, Ute Samtleben, Martina Giorgetti and Yari Presezzi of the Fatebenefratelli emergency room, ambulance drivers, and absolutely everyone on the staff of the Medicine 2 Ward at Sacco Hospital.

Next come those close to me and those who worried about me.

First and foremost, this includes Cristina, Tommaso, Alice and Tomasz, and my relatives and wonderful friends.

Many thanks also go out to all my patients, and especially Anna, for being there for me and for their support, patience and waiting for my return.

Thanks also to every person, near or far, who thought of me, before or after my illness – it was always appreciated.

And a special thank you to the readers of my story that appeared in the *il venerdì* insert – la Repubblica, for the appreciation and gratitude they showed.

Lastly, my heartfelt gratitude goes to Angelo Moroni for agreeing to share his experience with me, which was both different and similar to mine, and together with my contribution formed the basis of this book. I was truly lucky to be given a brother by Covid-19.

Introduction

Pietro Roberto Goisis and Antonio Angelo Moroni

The history of the coronavirus is short

The first cases mainly involved workers in the wet market in Wuhan, China, where fish and other animals were sold, including live animals. The first report attributable to the novel virus occurred on 31 December 2019, but the first patients with symptoms had already appeared earlier on 8 December. Some studies have suggested that the virus had been around since August 2019. On 1 January 2020, the authorities ordered the closure of the market and the isolation of those showing signs and symptoms of the infection. The first confirmed death was on 9 January 2020. In the first weeks of January 2020, scientists identified abnormal pneumonia in these subjects caused by a novel coronavirus, designated SARS-CoV-2 (*coronavirus 2 with severe acute respiratory syndrome*). The virus turned out to have at least 70% of its gene sequence similar to that of SARS-CoV. At the end of January 2020, the characteristics of the virus had not yet been well determined, although the ability to transmit from person to person was established, and uncertainties remained about the exact transmission methods and pathogenicity (the ability to cause harm). The associated disease was named COVID-19.

In Italy the virus was recognized in a daring way by Annalisa Manara, an anaesthesiologist at Codogno hospital, who, on the night between 19 and 20 February, and in violation of WHO guidelines (to test only those who had come in contact with individuals coming from China) isolated the first positive case in Italy, the mythical "Patient Zero", Mattia Maestri. When positive cases became public, politicians came into play, who were dumbfounded, unprepared and under pressure to perform. And then this alarming news became everyone's business. Feelings of fear, illness, death, sacrifice, the unknown and entrapment surfaced.

Everyone became painfully aware of the human, physical and psychological sacrifice of doctors and healthcare workers at all the hospitals in Lombardy, especially those in Bergamo and Brescia, not to mention primary care physicians, who were left alone to manage an area in which an unknown, highly dangerous virus was starting its unobstructed spread. This was a virus whose

DOI: 10.4324/9781003198734-1

2 Introduction

clinical course could lead to death, very quickly, even within a week, with no specific, proven treatments at that time to eradicate it.

Psychoanalysts, who were shut in their offices listening to their patients, and who, like everyone else, were completely unaware of what was happening at that time, grew concerned over how to act in the face of the danger of a contagion that was knocking at the door of their offices. Many of us provide psychotherapy to patients who are hospitalists. At that time there was a fierce debate among Italian colleagues about closing offices and making radical changes to the psychoanalytic setting, by shifting the therapeutic relationship to "remote" online platforms (e.g. WhatsApp, Skype, Zoom, Meet, etc.). This modality is already known and recognized by the international psycho-analytic community, but has so far only been "tolerated" for situations con-sidered exceptional, such as remote supervision of pupils living in areas far from organizations that provide psychoanalysis (e.g., residents in Asia or the Far East), or of patients already in analysis, but who had to move for reasons beyond their control. Suddenly changing the setting of all analyses became a real trauma for many psychoanalysts and for patients as well.

Stefano Bolognini is the former President of the International Psycho-analytical Association (IPA). In an IPA webinar on Covid-19 organized to discuss traumatic changes taking place during the most dramatic days of the contagion, he metaphorically described the emotional state of patients and analysts as "having been forced to move to a camp tent, after an earthquake that destroyed our homes, waiting for the police to take us back to inhabit our familiar surroundings". Most analysts have found themselves in this "camp tent" over the past few months. In this same context, a very heated debate has started in the Italian psychoanalytic community on "remote ana-lysis", as evidenced by the opening of the section "Internet- and phone-based analysis and psychotherapy at the time of the coronavirus" on Spiweb, the website of the Italian Psychoanalytic Society (SPI) (www.spiweb.it/area-diba ttiti/analisi-e-psicoterapie-internet-o-per-telefono-al-tempo-del-coronavirus/).

Angelo Antonio Moroni's "psychoanalytical diary" and Pietro Roberto Goisis's "clinical diary" are two different points of view (psychoanalytic and personal) in the same environment of the collective trauma experienced by the two authors during the epidemic that hit Italy (the first European country to be involved in this catastrophic experience). One is written by a psychoanalyst from his "camp tent", in which certain fundamental, time-tested procedures are suddenly questioned, and especially the setting. The other is the story of an analyst who came down with the Coronavirus, and who unwittingly had to return to being a patient, while keeping his analytical expertise alive and well (see the powerful description of the mutual therapeutic relationship between nurses and the patient–doctor in Roberto's diary). Thus, the two diaries share a painful and graphic account of how the trauma of the epidemic forced Ita-lian psychoanalysts to reconsider the issues of analytical "asymmetry" and "neutrality" – two different, but complementary, points of view.

Of course, the two authors are different in many ways. One lives and works in a small provincial town, Pavia, while the other in a large metropolis, Milan. They belong to different generations that separate them by about ten years (one is in his fifties and one in his sixties). Although they belong to the same psychoanalytic community (the Italian Psychoanalytic Society), Moroni's education is in psychology, while Goisis is an M.D. and psychiatrist.

Although there are differences, there are also several significant similarities and commonalities, and a certain degree of "intertwining" of life experiences that have gradually surfaced in the emotional side of their almost random encounter. For example, both work with adolescents, and for years this area has become the main field of their work and expertise. Angelo and Roberto also share a passion for the cinema and the positive way that the cinema and psychoanalysis influence each other. But writing is definitely also something that they have in common. "Writing" is understood as a form of practice and application, a way of thinking and creating to be considered, in a psychoanalytic context; and also as a function of emotional "literacy" that explores and deepens the "aesthetic paradigm" in psychoanalysis.

If we think back to these differences and commonalities between the two authors, certain overlaps and crossovers in their backgrounds appear that, despite their mutual substantial differences, now almost seem to be prophetic. In fact, despite any differences between the authors, the epidemic experience seems to have created some crossovers and, most importantly, a common feeling or "harmony", almost as if they had experienced a situation of "serendipitous" discovery. We realized, only later, for example, that, in parallel, and unbeknown to each other, on 10 March 2020 Angelo's diary, that of a psychoanalyst inside the lockdown, began, and on the same day Roberto's clinical diary covering the hospital and disease experience began.

These and other surprising coincidences remain in the subconscious of the authors allowing them to focus on more important and complex analytical tasks, but they have gradually surfaced when their backgrounds have crossed. Angelo started writing his diary by publishing a post on his Facebook page every day. Roberto saw these, read them, and was impressed by their ability to involve and draw readers in and tell a story. So when his own Covid storm had passed, he sent Angelo his own story, the first spontaneous version of the close, disturbing encounter with the virus. Since that time, which was about 4 April 2020, another remote dialogue has begun between them that they would now like to consolidate and bring to life in this book.

They were able to mix these key elements that characterized their meeting in such a particular way, but it would have been difficult for them to co-author a book, especially one on such a unique period and subject in human history. Perhaps it was precisely this exceptional situation that empowered them and created this opportunity.

Going back to the metaphor of the "camp tent" coined by Bolognini, while I, Angelo, wrote, day after day starting 10 March 2020, on my Facebook

4 Introduction

page, I thought of this psychoanalytic diary as a "war diary", just as I thought of my office, devoid of patients, as the "camp tent" that Bolognini refers to. The crackling of the computer audio that brought me the voices of my patients, who were in turn home-bound due to the government-imposed quarantine, reminded me of military radio transmissions in World War II. Or truck drivers, who in the solitude of the truck's cockpit, racing down cold, grey highways, seek out a human voice on their radios, a contact with their fellow truckers. During almost three months of lockdown, it was hard to stay away from patients, and to share with them the sense of helplessness and pain they felt. I am referring in particular to the many doctors who I followed day after day via Skype, all working on the front in devastated wards converted into Covid-19 areas, who risked their lives and put their family members at risk. This diary talks a lot about them, and I realize that it conveys a certain amount of anguish, because it was usually written at the end of the day, after having taken in and listened to the agonies of death told by different health-care workers committed to fighting the virus who have seen many patients die on their watch. It really felt like war.

While Angelo was writing "his" diary, I, Roberto, in a similar way, began to put together the pieces of the story, "my" clinical diary, that of a psychoanalyst who was torn away from work and daily life by the brutally violent virus. I too have inhabited a sort of camp tent, not because the hospital where I was hospitalized was not properly equipped, but because the novelty of the disease, the healthcare industry's ignorance of its manifestations and the absence of clinical evidence on the most effective treatments really made me feel like I was in an emergency. When I actually left that tent, I was able to resume my profession as a psychoanalyst, meet with patients and colleagues again, and somehow work with Angelo and become one of the protagonists in his diary.

We dedicate our diaries to the doctors and healthcare workers whose fate we followed for about three months in addition to all the people who, on the other side of the barricade, suffered from the pandemic. To the many, too many people, who didn't make it. To way too many patients who together with their doctors fought tooth and nail to get treatment. To the relatives of the sick who were isolated like their loved ones, and waited hellish days and nights for phone calls and updates. To those who lost their loved ones and were not even able to say good-bye to them. And to all our compatriots who suffered from the repercussions that impacted their freedom, work, relationships and emotions. A particular thought also goes out to the many adolescents we have listened to during all these long days of quarantine. These young people showed us their rooms and living environments online, allowing us to enter, because of the virus, their intimate private mental and physical spaces. As psychoanalysts, but also as citizens and human beings in general, we will need a long time to process the trauma we have all experienced. We hope that these diaries represent a small, personal and thus, authentic contribution to this end.

Chapter 1

Psychoanalytic diary in the lockdown

Angelo Antonio Moroni

Day one   10th March 2020

A day on the battleground. At 8 a.m. my wife is admitted to the San Matteo Polyclinic: every member of staff is wearing masks and gloves. They won't let me in. "Maybe tomorrow" – they tell me – "at 12, but only for a few minutes". A long day follows on Skype with almost all of my patients. The last Skype session traumatizes me. It's with a patient of mine, an internist, who arrives at the session after 11 consecutive days of work, exhausted. He feel's as if he's on duty at a war front. He has seen an average of five patients a day die in 20 days, only in his ward, when the average is usually three deaths a month, all with severe and very severe respiratory diseases. The anaesthesiologist on his ward last week told him to call him only for patients 75 and under. He says use morphine to "to assist the others as they die". This week the anaesthetist's guidelines change: "Call me only for patients aged 65 and under." There are no more beds, ventilators are scarce. My patient tells me "He understands that taking away the ventilator from a patient who is talking, but can choke to death, to give it to someone more serious than him, is a difficult decision". Then he adds, "I can assure you that medicine in this case can do nothing". Moreover, he continues, the government has decreed to remove the Criminal Responsibility of doctors. This has never happened before, perhaps only in times of war. But, he adds, they don't talk about this on the news. They're using antiviral drugs used for AIDS and special molecules used for the Ebola virus. I feel traumatized, like my patient. I had been too optimistic. And my wife is having surgery tomorrow. In a hospital. And they'll only let me in for a few minutes. I'm reminded of Bion, his "War Memories". I'm helping my patient write his war memoirs. I'm helping myself write mine.

Day two

Second day. I'm kept waiting outside the ward for two hours, waiting for my wife to come out of surgery: the hysterical nurses give me precise orders "Put

DOI: 10.4324/9781003198734-2

your mask on", they tell me. "Absolutely use the sanitizer gel. You can only go into the room for ten minutes." My wife is fine, she's just recovering from the anaesthesia, and we are reassured by the fact that we know the anaesthetist. We are moved by the solidarity we receive from many colleagues and friends who work at San Matteo. "I'm here if you need me", says my colleague, a psychiatrist of the hospital, also overwhelmed by the management of an SPDC[1] in fibrillation. Meanwhile I hear the sound of helicopters above our heads. We have stopped counting the ambulance sirens, but I've been hearing them blasting with an incredibly unusual frequency also from home, for the past several days now. While I am with my wife, after exactly ten minutes, a brusque female voice on the ward speakers announces: "Relatives are invited to leave the ward immediately." I have time to have a word with my wife, relieved that the surgery went well. A day follows with seven patients on Skype, including some doctors who are always rather distressed and in need of psychological support. One of them tells me about his elderly father who has a cough and possibly Covid symptoms. Another psychiatrist colleague then tells me that she has to manage three SPDCs at the same time due to lack of staff. Before going to sleep my son Alessandro invites me to watch a beautiful horror movie together that is being streamed: *The Witch*, set in seventeenth-century New England, set during the same period of Manzoni's plague. I accept with pleasure.

Day three

After three Skype sessions with teenagers talking to me about everything but Covid-19, i.e. school, boyfriends and girlfriends that they broke up with, artistic gymnastics, juvenile acne, homosexuality, heterosexuality and bisexuality, and other similar vital epiphanies, three more online sessions with three truly "frontline" doctors follow. One of them describes his day in Milan at a call centre organized by the Order of Psychologists of Lombardy. The service is run by psychiatrists and psychologists and is aimed at helping medical staff in the Coronavirus trench. A psycho-traumatological service, practically, managed by volunteer professionals. My patient tells me, for example, about a nurse who calls him and who does not want to go back to work because she is tired of seeing dead people every day. The second patient, a doctor in a private facility, tells me that her mind is "too full": soon a decree will mandate that her ward will be totally dedicated to the care of Covid-19 patients. But the problem is that they are not used to treating this type of patients. They are not pneumologists, nor anaesthetists. The head of the department is tormented, and the FFP2 and FFP3 masks have not yet arrived. Will they arrive? One of her colleagues from Bergamo tells her that many people are dying in that hospital. They can't take it anymore. The third Skype session is with another doctor, in quarantine at home because he came into contact with a positive case. He has a cough. His wife and children live in the same home with him, but he must stay separated from them: they must avoid any contact whatsoever. At the end of the day, I recall the first three adolescent patients with nostalgia, and their wonderful juvenile acne. Tomorrow, fortunately, is Friday.

Day four

My doctor patient tells me, via Skype, that he is tired, not only emotionally, but also physically: this week he has done an average of 15 hospitalizations per day, all for Covid-19 pathologies. It will be long, he tells me, the curve is not logarithmic, but exponential. All three of the hospital's floors of Medicine have been used for virus-positive patients. These sessions are very heavy for me. I feel like I'm talking online to an astronaut orbiting another, inhospitable and dangerous planet. He tells me that for every patient admitted, he has to remove his personal protective equipment, take off his visor, glasses, gloves, wash himself, throw everything away and get dressed for the next admission. The mechanical ventilators are missing. A colleague of his tried to invent one by assembling pieces of other instruments, helping the patients breathe, and then transferring them to the intensive care unit. "You know when you put the Lego bricks together? That's what my colleague did. But it worked. But this makes you realize how desperate we are." He also tells me that by now he feels that he's not curing the patients but assisting them, which for a doctor means having lost his weapons. Someone, something, has suddenly taken them away from him. In the intensive care unit of his hospital there were eight beds, now there are 20. Today, the resuscitator colleague, after 20 days of intubating patients in desperate conditions, finally managed to remove the respirator from a seriously ill 53-year-old woman, who is now breathing on her own. The whole team applauds and everyone starts crying. The woman looks at them in amazement and doesn't understand what is happening. "I've never seen such a thing in a medical team before." I feel like crying when he tells me this story, I'm really touched by it and I tell him. This is what another patient, a psychiatrist, who works in a psycho-traumatology call centre, tells me. He's scared, he had a cough today and wants to go for a chest X-ray. Both of them don't seem to be very optimistic about the ongoing crisis. "It's gonna take a long time", they all tell me. Barricaded in my office today I heard an ambulance siren about every ten minutes. It will be long, I think. It will be long.

Day five

It's finally Saturday. So to say because I spent the whole day speaking to colleagues from various parts of Italy via Skype and on the phone. We are discussing with them this blessed matter regarding the virtual setting and other scientific issues, but there is also family, friendship and affection. Alessandro invites me to do a 2 km run in the countryside and it does wonders for my body and my spirit. I don't dare venture in supermarkets or any other kind of meeting places. Michele is also stuck at home and plays online with his friends and chats on the phone with his girlfriend, I think; he deserves more at 19. In the evening we gather around the TV to watch the film *Oblivion* with Tom Cruise and the great Morgan Freeman. A post-apocalyptic film which is very much in tune with these times we are living in. I think to myself that what we need are representations: "visions", dreams, narratives and reveries.

Day six

It's a quiet Sunday. I pass the day having many Skype video calls with colleagues and friends trying to understand how to adjust a therapeutic container forcibly deformed by the raw and aggressive reality of the virus. I reflect a lot on the inherent transformation of the classic analytic setting and unpleasantly moving away from the analytic device designed by Freud. The setting is in fact an interweaving between the "analytic site" (analyst's study, how the patient gets there, the time of the session, physical aspect of the couch) and the "analysing situation" (analytic process itself, dialectic transference/countertransference, role of the body, non-verbal in session, enactment, etc.). Where will all this end up on Skype, I wonder? And what about the fact that I see the patient's home through the webcam? This is a truly unprecedented situation, but perhaps it helps us better grasp the meaning of the "unconscious".

Day seven

I prefer writing about more pleasant things, but these days, it is probably far beyond my scope. These days I seem to experience what Bollas describes as "the return of the oppressed" (Bollas, 2018), not "the repressed, mind you", but the "oppressed". An oppressed humanity that returns, and that we had forgotten, rejected, but that returns to knock on the door of our unresolved mourning. A colleague from Milan writes to me about a friend of his from Bergamo, 75 years old, with a fever of 40 for two weeks, diagnosed with coronavirus together with his wife and who is staying at home: they told him that there is no room at the hospital. He can only go to the Emergency Room if he has serious difficulties breathing, and they tell him to only take paracetamol. His wife improved after a week and now she is assisting him, because when they were both sick, they were alone and couldn't have any help. The doctors, their friends, strongly advised against hospitalization because there is no room. Now, how many people has this man infected before he started having the symptoms, my colleague wonders? At the end of the day Michele sent me the poem "Loneliness" by Eugenio Montale on WhatsApp. "These verses suit this historical moment", he says to me.

Day eight

I spend an average of 7–8 hours a day on Skype, equivalent to the same number of sessions I do. My eyes are starting to hurt from prolonged exposure to the screen, and so are my ears, because of the earphones. My calves are also starting to hurt as well as my lumbar vertebrae, because I have stopped playing tennis which is my favourite sport and I sit all day in front of the computer listening to the anguish of doctors (today there were four), hysterical mothers with children at home from school (two), psychologists who have had to interrupt the internships they just started (one). A 25-year-old patient this afternoon tells me with sadness that she has had a fever of 38° C for three days and a sore throat. She lives with her boyfriend and maybe she got it from him because he works in a supermarket. She has to work overtime and is out all day in contact with many colleagues. My bones chill when she tells me that, coughing from the monitor. Whenever possible, I go out between one patient and another and I walk as long as possible, at a fast pace, with Dylan, to try to relax my legs and try to avoid a postural collapse. Luckily behind my office there is boundless countryside and I feel privileged to be out in the open air without meeting anyone. I look around myself in the countryside and everything seems frozen, still, although Dylan is running around looking for pheasants. I think of friends and colleagues who have offices in Milan, Genoa, Modena, Rome, who would never be able to have a long hour of fresh air.

Day nine

Today is the first time since the beginning of all this wretched collective tragedy that I begin to feel a profound sense of helplessness, as if I'm facing something much bigger than myself. I think of *Moby Dick* by Melville. I feel like Ishmael, at the mercy of the destructive forces exerted on him by an irrepressible Captain Ahab, as he guides the *Pequod* through the waves of a dangerous ocean. Now I don't get much relief, not even when I go out with my dog in the country alone. Too much silence. Too much emptiness. A sense of darkness. That's it, darkness. As if I'd walked into a room with no light and groped around blindly, but this is the same dark room where I must take my patients by the hand, guide them and reassure them. I'm guiding children in the dark, but I'm also guiding the child in me in the dark. This image has crossed my mind in various Skype sessions today, especially with some teenagers. One of them "let me into" her room (I can see her face-to-face), and I thank her for that: the room of a teenager is a sacred and inviolable place, and she let me in, with a smile tinged with sadness. "I spend a lot of time in my room", she says to me, "sometimes I put things in order, but in these days I'm using this time to put things in order inside myself." I feel honoured, but at the same time frightened and, at the same time, helpless: I have to guide her in this darkness that we are all experiencing. "But I'm lucky", she tells me again, "in summer, when it's hot I have a balcony and I go outside with my computer and watch a movie." "Like a drive-in, but a bit 'bonsai'", I reply, and she smiles at me. She should be watching a movie on a balcony on a summer night with someone else rather than by herself.

Day ten

I think that this epidemic will sign our souls. Some people call it "the Self", but theoretical distinctions don't matter these days. Tonight I was talking on the phone with a colleague about the fact that it will take years to emotionally process this tragic moment we are experiencing. In analysis I see new disturbing objects, dense with polysemic meanings, distributed on several planes exhibiting various gradients of anguish, metaphorized by inanimate objects that transmit the feelings conveyed by these experiences. One of these new analytic "characters" is the C-PAP, the "positive pressure mechanical ventilator", which seems like a plastic diver's helmet which is used in resuscitation to insufflate oxygen in respiratory failure. I'm becoming an expert on these issues in spite of myself: some of the doctors in the trenches, during their sessions, tell me how it works, how it is a real torture for some patients during resuscitation because they feel like suffocating for at least ten minutes after it is removed. "Then it passes", one of my doctor patients tells me, "but we have to sedate them in almost all cases: otherwise, they try to tear them off. We usually use it in rare cases. Even seeing ten patients in a room like this is something else." Once again I have the same haunting thoughts this mass tragedy will leave its sign on us. One of my dearest friends, a psychotherapist who lives in the tormented area between Bergamo and Brescia, makes me think so too. She writes to me that she had a dream that upset her. She feels the need to share this dream with me and, I'm very grateful to her, gives me permission to write it here. It shows us how our unconscious, our frightened, helpless Self, is already changing. My colleague writes to me:

> I dreamt I was being chased by men who wanted to hurt me, I was running with a newborn baby in my arms. I entered a church with the newborn baby to find shelter, I tried to enter the confessional hoping there was only a priest. Instead, besides the priest, there was an oriental man that I asked to leave always keeping a safe distance from him and in the meanwhile, I stayed in there with the priest and the newborn baby in my arms. But then in reality I come home from work and I see my daughter in the distance studying just outside the front door so that she could stay in the open air. Then I feel better notwithstanding the persistent dense silence out there interrupted solely and exclusively by ambulance sirens that I no longer count.

All this will change us. It already has changed us. Maybe because all of this has already happened. But over the years we have forgotten it, and now we have been forced to remember it.

Day eleven

Today has been relatively peaceful. I exchange emails with colleagues talking about Sophocles' Antigone, about Creonte, about restrictions of freedom. I think we're experiencing some kind of induced agoraphobia. Like everyone else, I have had to restrict my movements to what is absolutely necessary: I only go out two or three mornings a week to buy the newspaper, with a mask. I avoid supermarkets, also because my immune system is not particularly equipped. When I was 40 years old I had chickenpox, which left me with an annoying case of Herpes Zoster which re-emerges every two or three years giving me irritating shingles and corneal herpes which I combat with tons of antiviral medication. My general practitioner keeps telling me to keep safe and I agree with him. Fortunately, my doctor patient who works in the most dangerous "trench" was more serene today. He told me that they finally received sufficient supplies of oxygen, which was running out, even though the oxygen systems didn't hold up, so he had to move all the beds to the ground floor. He told me: "Usually the system can handle 4 litres of oxygen per minute per patient. Now we need about 80 litres per minute, and the number of patients has increased fivefold." Good thing we have the hyperbaric chamber for the analysis, I think to myself. It seems like the oxygen system in my office is holding up well. I'm glad.

Day twelve

My viburnums have blossomed, as have the hellebores. The hydrangeas that I planted in the big garden next to the ground floor front door are sprouting leaves. I spent half an afternoon watering all the plants and taking care of them: this hobby of mine relaxes me, especially on Saturdays or Sundays. I love homemaking activities, like cooking when I have time – I don't have much time – because now I dedicate some hours to watching the English TV series *Broadchurch*, which I recommend, as well as to reading newspapers. I'd say it's been a rather restful day. Then I find out that just recently a colleague who is not old, more or less my age from Lombardy has been hospitalized in intensive care. Fortunately, he is better now, but he was hardly breathing and they had to ventilate him for several days. So now I find myself thinking Covid-19 is also now amongst us, it has reached the homes of psychoanalysts. I also think that everything that is happening is a huge narcissistic wound for us. We have long denied seeing our human frailty, an incontrovertible truth, but clouded by the illusion that we could do anything: go anywhere, buy everything we desired on Amazon, illuded that we had triumphed over Nature.

12 Angelo Antonio Moroni

Now it is as if we discover that the earth is not flat, but round, and that it revolves around the sun. A real traumatic mental Copernican revolution. A change of perspective that we didn't expect, and that overwhelms us now in its total factuality. That makes us see what Heidegger would call our "throwness" in the world. My viburnums are not touched by this bitter awareness, and neither are my hydrangeas, nor the hellebores that I keep on the terrace.

Day thirteen

I spend this Sunday online with many friends and family. We share scientific articles by virologists, biologists, philosophers. Everything and more in order to try to generate a "beam of intense darkness" and sustain an emotional–affective unison while changing geometries and perspectives are disrupting our contacts and relationships. Two of our dearest and long-time friends "invite us to dinner" on Skype on Monday or Tuesday evening. I will finish late with my sessions but I am happy to create a small agora to limit the effects of isolation and promote a sense of continuity and familiarity. We are equipping ourselves in the attempt to keep creativity and mental life alive. I try to do the same thing with my patients. A great suggestion that I immediately followed came from my friend and colleague Luca Trabucco from Genoa who thought of putting the laptop on the couch, with the webcam facing the wall in front, so that the patients in session see what is familiar to their eyes when they lie down on the couch. Everyone really appreciated this "setting variation" inside the already complicated variation of the overall setting. New internal and external geometries are forming, and I think about what effects this is producing on our minds and will produce as time passes which in itself "the perception of the passage of time" is also changing. In the meantime, I receive requests from various journalists asking me for interviews and psychoanalytic opinions on this moment and on this unknown land we are all crossing over together. It seems that everyone is looking for a "beam of intense darkness". It reminds me of the image of Pinocchio seeing Geppetto's lighted candle afar, illuminating the belly of the whale. I feel the need for a stable reference point that can be a heart-warming affection and that can furnish meaning, in the middle of an immense, unknown and claustrophobic ocean.

Day fourteen

I realize that every day, or rather, at the end of the day, it is as if my mind needs to isolate "selected facts", "model scenes", "gestalt" of the analytic day just ended, in order to better represent the emotions I experienced. I imagine that this mental work is an essential component of my analytic function, of the analytic function of all analysts in general. Also this space in the evening dedicated to writing this diary is gradually assuming this function: a way of mending a tear, of this traumatic separation; my patients so far away, I am really beginning to miss their physical presence, but at the same time, and for the same reason they are so close, sharing an absence/presentation that bears the sign of an unknown overwhelming us and violently standing between us, and imposing itself on our desire to meet. Today is Monday: here we go again, I think of how the morning will be. All the sessions hinge on individual variations of a general theme, on that particular "chosen fact" regarding restrictions, losses, changes in daily proxemic boundaries, and on modifications in the perception of space and time. All the sessions focus on new emotions that were never experienced before, especially the need to reorganize one's own living space, of living and inhabiting one's own home and oneself. I am particularly struck by the story of a young patient of mine who has three small children, the oldest of whom is seven years old. She lives in a two-room apartment. She and her husband are now both at home smart working. The grandparents live in another town that cannot be reached by government decree. "Yesterday I took them to the basement near the garage driveway of the apartment building. At least they had more space to play", the patient tells me, "We don't even have a condominium garden, and this is the twelfth day we have been almost completely locked in the house. From today it will be worse ...". I think we are living an experience that has something philosophical about it, a truly epochal moment, then I find myself thinking maybe I'm being too intellectual which is certainly my defence mechanism against emotions that are difficult for me to "digest". The book by Pier Aldo Rovatti *Abitare la distanza* (Living the distance) comes to mind – all day long. A book that talks about the human condition and its fundamental paradox: man is inside and outside, close and at the same time always elsewhere. He needs a place, a "home" to stay in, for shelter, but then, as soon as he finds this place he has so long desired, he then discovers the importance of being "outside", of the "open", of distance, of the Alterity, which is never where he would like it to be. Today, the sessions were full of this absence/presence.

Day fifteen

After 15 days of Skype sessions, I begin to show some signs of fatigue. Before the tsunami-Covid I used remote methodology only for patients living abroad, who are few compared to the overall percentage of patients I follow. I am not used to this type of setting and I find it tiring. After lunch I have to stop and sleep for half an hour before resuming my afternoon work in the studio. It's never happened to me before. I never needed to do so until now. It had never happened to me before 10th March. My patients seem to be divided into two different categories: the first one only talks about the pandemic, obviously especially the doctors, and even more obviously, the doctors on the front line; the second category is made up of younger patients, who as soon as we are online, vis-à-vis or on the virtual couch, talk about something totally different, immediately resuming the train of thought where they left off in the previous session. In both categories, however, I see a common train of thought, which is that of separation, intertwined with that of emotional dependence, presented in all the possible nuances imaginable, from sentimental memories to those of the "good old times", now gone, now lost, whether it be childhood, or adolescence, middle school, old photos that suddenly reveal new lights and evoking both old and new emotions. It's as if the words of the patients contained and manifested, discrete, continuous are but constant epiphanies constituting what I would try to define as a "previous ulteriority". Something lost that returns under a new ghostly guise. I suddenly see the patients, as never before, as if they were monuments of memories, as never before, speaking to me from a sonorous elsewhere that continuously enters my ears through the earphones connected to Skype. Enigmatic Moai very far away, on their Easter Island, and at the same time very close, by the voice far too loud amplified by the sound card of the pc.

Day sixteen

I went out with Dylan after dinner, and as soon as I walked out the front door I was hit by a blast of unexpected icy wind. It's been a long day, and I have tried to make it as pleasant as possible, for example by signing up for the IPA webinar on Friday, 27th March with speakers including Stefano Bolognini, and other colleagues from the US, Latin America and a Chinese psychoanalyst, from whom I'm very interested in hearing about Covid-19, of course. Also on Friday another webinar on isolation stress and "allostatic load", a concept that intrigues me due to its fascinating polysemics. Then I use WhatsApp to talk with two or three colleagues about the new Austrian Netflix series on Freud. It's really horrendous and must be totally avoided, I think I'll write a terrible review because it doesn't deserve anything more. It is, basically, a good day too, even if dominated, like the previous ones, by an unnatural sense of numbness, as if we were buried by 10 feet of snow, that fell all in one night. I write to my general practitioner – a friend I have known for thirty years – to find out how he is: he tells me that he receives about a hundred phone calls a day, plus emails and various messages, He says that he would love to have a chat with me because he is at this limit. But he can't, he doesn't have time to talk to his friends. This time I avoid talking about other doctors on Skype, or about colleagues and friends who tell me about boyfriends or companions or relatives hospitalized or with fevers, but my impression today is that this "enemy" is getting closer, considering that more and more people close to me have relatives that are infected or presenting somewhat suspicious symptoms … I imagine that this thought comes from the "allostatic load". Going out in the evening with Dylan, however, consoles me a bit.

Day seventeen

The patients and I are getting used to our remote Skype sessions. I am gathering and recording verbal and non-verbal elements which all give me positive feedback about them, and they will help me when I reflect on this forcibly varied setting in the future. "I lay down on the couch this time, with my laptop on my legs, so I feel like I'm on your couch", a patient tells me this morning, "and I have a picture of the wall of your office in front of me and I look at the window that I usually see when I'm there. I was much more relaxed during this session, more than others." These are small "discoveries", small somatic and intrapsychic adjustments that we are gradually learning together, just like we are learning that it takes time, as Piaget says, to assimilate and adapt to the new conditions. Voices, for example, seem to take on different weights, the same goes for the silences, which I feel are different from those in a normal analytic interaction in flesh and blood. It's as if the voice arrives closer instantaneously, albeit from a distant subject, and hence is somehow more invasive and moving. This implies thinking about creating different modulations, different cadences, a different analytic musicality, touching new internal strings of both members of the analytic couple at work. Today, for example, I caught myself interpreting a transference that referred to the role played by Skype. It was in fact the first time this happened to me, and I think I will even have to study this aspect as well. It seems to me that distance, the impossibility of a "real" contact, seems to be becoming less of a problem, no longer such a cumbersome object.

But patients are not the only persons I contact remotely, but also friends and relatives who are far away and in quarantine. For example, I use WhatsApp to speak to my nephew, who lives and works in Paris. He tells me that last week it was really hard to be isolated alone in his home, but this week he's getting used to it, and then he can work remotely from there. I also have many other nieces and nephews and their children in Paris, a city that I love for this very reason, and where I wanted to go at Easter to visit them, all these dear young relatives: however the current pandemic circumstances have caused this dream to fade away. But I am more than certain that dreams resist and will resist any virus: I am more than certain.

Day eighteen

Continuity seems to be the "selected fact" of today. I organized a meeting on Zoom with some colleagues from Milan: we all felt the need to give continuity to the groups where we talk about clinical cases and have been doing so for more than 10 years at the home of a very hospitable Milanese colleague. Then we have lunch together and everyone brings something to eat, for example Genoese farinata, some cheese, and I usually bring a cake or homemade bread. We work for about two hours on the cases, then we chat, we talk about our children, the books we are reading, the films we have seen. On 6th April, then another group, even larger, of the Milanese Centre of Psychoanalysis "Cesare Musatti", my original training school, always on Zoom: there will be at least 20 analysts. I think we all will have a lot of things to share, and we will feel the nostalgia of that place. We miss those corridors, now empty and silent, the paintings with black and white photographs by Luciana Nissim Momigliano, by Cesare Musatti with that sly smile painted on his lips, his white hair, and the room with the fireplace, with the print of Adami with the orange couch, the balcony overlooking that ugly outdoor courtyard, the poster depicting Eugenio Gaburri, my teacher and one of my first supervisors, other photos of Giuseppe Pellizzari, a dear friend and late teacher. I think we will all have many thoughts and memories that we will share on Zoom, that will be expressed by the wrinkles on our faces lit by the webcam LED, while we access the meeting room, disembodied, but alive in our stories, in our battles, in our very diverse ways of groping in the dark, in our attempt to touch what is trying, that surface from the depths of these unknown sea beds that we are crossing.

Day nineteen

Maybe because it's Saturday, maybe because it's sunny and the temperature has pleasantly increased, but today I really miss playing tennis, I miss forehands and backhands, I miss the clay court and sweating after a game and the pleasant sensation I feel in my muscles after playing. I've loved tennis since I was 12 years old, ever since I first played in the courtyard below my house, with my middle school friends. At that time, we still used wooden rackets, which were very heavy to handle. I've always enjoyed this sport and I've always played except for a long pause, which lasted during my University years, until 2005, when I took it up again, continuously as an amateur. This space I dedicate to play is fundamental for me, where I rediscover my body, that preadolescent sensory function I lost, since I have always done such an intellectual and "rickety" job. Now this rickety sensation is accentuated by this forced seclusion. For many years now, this space dedicated entirely to myself had always been a part of every weekend. Now it has been taken away from me. These free associations deriving from my own personal story, make me think of the very recent stories I've heard from some adolescent patients, who have just begun to experience new bodily sensations, with the need to express and explore their developing sexuality, new sentimental relationships in which discovering one's own body and that of the other was leading to increasingly vital changes. This epiphany was now interrupted, compressed. Some saw fading relations with their "first boyfriend" fade away, others had just resumed their shy contacts with friends and social networks that they had abandoned for various reasons, still others were planning to start living with their new loves. A young patient began to describe the emotion of the first kiss, a coveted surge, but that truly unsettled him, feeling as if a current of tenderness had been now swept away and postponed indefinitely. With the Skype audio interference in the background, a girl describes to me the joyful yet contemporarily disturbing intensity, of the "carnal passion" she feels towards her new partner, now brought in an unknown and sidereal ether. Sometimes they cry together from their monitors: they want to be together, but they can't. Bodies, sexuality, tenderness are suspended and stripped away. The right to express their vitality is now frozen and denied. Bodies that remind me of abjection and illness. Bodies that no longer convey the need for intimacy. "Intimacy" is one of my favourite English terms, and which I believe really renders what I mean. Today is Saturday which gives me time to balance and counterbalance the weight of my reflections, under an invigorating, warm sun, walking in the fields behind my house, with Dylan and his friend Ginger, my neighbour's little Irish setter just like him. Seeing them running at breakneck speed in the green, sunny, deserted fields gives me a sense of fresh vitality. I would like to see my young patients running and hugging each other around the world as they look out onto this currently uncertain future. And I would love to imagine myself on the tennis court, with clouds of red dirt flying up as I slide sideways to attempt a backspin.

Day twenty

A Sunday full of artistic things, creativity, music, cinema, singing, cooking. After lunch, my wife and I are singing Battisti's songs at the top of our lungs, in the living room, in a strange surge of off-key exhilaration, but we may be feel the need to express a sign, a dream, and share yearning for freedom and life. We don't often use YouTube but sometimes, it seems to help us to find a relational pathos especially in these days that other thoughts dominate our horizon alternating between looming darkness and hesitant nuances of hope. A wave of emotions, that come and go, rise and fall again in this glasshouse-home. At times we seem to perceive it as if it were a bonsai garden, but the miniature pots are supposed to contain very big plants, and there is not even an expert Japanese gardener to properly take care of it. I spent the afternoon, instead, talking about movies with my friend director Giorgio Magarò, on Skype. We also spoke of the reviews of his new short film that will be released on 4th April. It's always nice to talk to Giorgio: today on Skype we share ideas, comment about trailers, and we talk about the director of *Parasite*, Bong Joon Ho, his other great films, *The Host, Mother, Snowpiercer, Memoir of an Assassin*, then we get onto techniques of writing screenplays. He reads a piece of his last short film. He asks me for my opinion, I ask him for opinions. Then I confess to him that I've always dreamed of writing and shooting the screenplay for a horror film, a "rural Gothic", like the novels by Eraldo Baldini, do you remember his book *Children, Spiders and Other Predators*?

In the evening the whole family is gathered around the TV to watch Ridley Scott's *The Martian*, which is always great, always good. This makes me think of the Swiss sculptor Hans Ruedi Giger who Scott commissioned to make the shapes of Alien, while Ridley gave the French designer Jean Giraud, better known as Moebius, the job of designing the costumes of the human astronauts. The director specifically chose two different artists to represent Alien and the Humans, so that the two different worlds depicted would truly be as different as possible. I really think we need another Giger to depict this devious enemy that is invading us. The weekend is over, tomorrow is Monday and I'm going to dive deep into other universes, other dreams, other drawings, and I hope I will have the company of Moebius, and of the images of the survivor on Mars in Ridley Scott's film. After all, we will all be survivors after this scourge.

Day twenty-one

Very sad, very sad indeed. Fausto Petrella left us today. Sadness is added to sadness. One of the founding fathers of Italian Psychoanalysis and Psychiatry, I had known him for about 40 years and had met him for the first time when I was only 18 in his beautiful house in the centre of Pavia, upon invitation by Silvia and Laura, his daughters, my lifelong friends. For me, then a teenager, he was one of the first examples representing a rigorous, vital, militant and, passionate way of doing psychoanalysis, which led me to follow that path, that interest in the unconscious but also in art and creativity, which brought me here now. The "mind as a theatre" has always been one of his favourite metaphors to describe our mind, full of characters and identifications which can be moved and removed in the course of our lives. I had spoken to him on the phone in January, we talked about his book *L'ascolto e l'ostacolo*, a very refined essay on psychoanalysis and music, and he had complimented me on my book *On the Uncanny*, "a very topical and useful subject to take up", he had told me. I attended so many of his seminars at the Collegio Nuovo in Pavia during my years at university, and then later during my psychiatric work at the Fatebenefratelli Institute in San Colombano al Lambro. Then there were the lessons he gave in Milan, at the Milanese Centre of Psychoanalysis "Cesare Musatti". So many, too many memories are crowding my mind today. And then, after a WhatsApp message arrives in the evening from Silvia, which shakes me up and pierces me with a sharp stab of pain.

Day twenty-two

I notice that I am starting to reason with my patients about the "temporariness" of this new virtual setting. Working helps me to elaborate this collective mourning, as well as my personal mourning, and above all that for Fausto Petrella, who I think of constantly between one patient and another. Like when I saw him coming out of his office located in a house in Pavia, between one patient and another and meeting up with a group of us to talk about politics. Then he would leave with his mocking smile and greet us with a closed fist: this is the most vivid and combative image of his that accompanies me. It was 1982. Today's sessions all focus on the desire to be here in my studio with me, in flesh and blood, hinting at the possibility that I and the patients could slip into a somewhat ghostly, semi-hallucinatory drift, a hypnagogic couple state without even noticing it. The analyst is asked, between the lines, to look out for this possibility, as if the "free associations" ran the risk of becoming free "dissociations", as if this temporary dissociation between an absent body and an overwhelming voice and monitor could refer to other parts of our dissociated Selves to integrate, to think and to dream. This is what a young patient of mine says to me: "It seems as if I'm living a situation of a dislocated body, as when one gets out of one's own body and sees it from afar, you know, like in certain science fiction films." Exactly, pure science fiction, I think, only it's real, very real. And this is where the concept of the "temporariness" comes in, which I feel is reassuring, limiting, soothing. A patient would like to go against the government restrictions and bring me the fee: "at least in the mailbox, so I can see the walls of your office." Luckily, he is only a kilometre away from me and he is a doctor, so he is permitted to move. We reflect on his need for "everything to pass soon" and "to finally return home". We reflect on the use of Skype, on technology, and its effects on the analytic process, on the cracking audio, on what was there before and is no longer now, on the rhythm of the sessions that "thank goodness that at least this is left", on the "fort–da", on what is transformed and what remains, on the "created–found" object.

Day twenty-three

I find myself having fantasies of uninhabited worlds, like in the novel *I Am Legend* by Richard Matheson. I talk at length with a patient on Skype about this author who also knows him: he is a young patient who loves science fiction and writes short stories. He tells me about a new novel he's writing. He is also writing a daily diary, like me – but he doesn't know it – it is the story of a survivor in a post-apocalyptic world. "I organize my days by studying in the morning and writing in the afternoon, so I try to give a rhythm to time, so that the weekend is different from the week. On weekends I watch movies and TV series." I feel like I really ended up in a science fiction movie, in a TV series. With this patient, in particular, the boundary between reality and fiction is always very blurred in truth, his narrations usually describe sidereal, empty, autistic worlds, but at least he tells them to me, like daydreams. "Tell me if I'm boring you", he says sometimes, and it is very endearing. He doesn't bore me at all, but his words suddenly seem prophetic to me. I find deafening silence every rare time I go out, to take my dog, and myself, out. I don't see anyone around, I don't hear a noise, not a car, at any time of the day. And to think that my studio is a stone's throw away from a big shopping mall, always full of people. These days the parking lot is semi-deserted, I never meet a soul. As if everyone had left. As if the earth was no longer inhabited by the human species. I speak to friends all over the world and they all have the same feeling. From Paris, Africa, the

United States, everyone I speak to has a tone of despondency that leaks out in their voices, despite their efforts to hold it back: they are barricaded in their homes as if the world outside had stopped and turned into a great silent pneumatic vacuum. Many films come to mind: *The Day After*, for example, one of the first catastrophic films that tries to describe the atomic risk and its consequences. The sense of time seems to change, closed as we are in our fragile anti-atomic bunkers. Last night, for example, I slept for almost nine hours in a row, like a rock, since I felt extremely tired after a day of work in this strange "new world": it hadn't happened to me since university times.

Day twenty-four

"We are not heroes, we just want to work safely and avoid being vectors for the virus", he tells me, around 7.30 p.m., the last patient of the day, a doctor in the trenches, with some of his relatives hospitalized and some of them intubated in intensive care wards scattered throughout Lombardy. There were no more places closer to home. I spend the day between sessions and meetings on Zoom with colleagues. We all talk about how, in this moment, we feel extremely frail in a very subjective and individual way and we wonder if we transmit these feelings to the patients and also whether or not we should hide or minimize these feelings, these concerns of ours. All of us – there are seven of us on Zoom – agree that it makes no sense to minimize, that we too are not heroes either, that omnipotent fathers don't exist and that perhaps this could be an opportunity to work on the sense of omnipotence as a defence against the anguish and intrinsic fragility that distinguishes us as human beings. As my patient will tell me later: "There is no Superman or Spiderman here. We must just go on sailing by sight: now the doctors that have come to work with me in this emergency come all from different wards and fields, the resources are few and many doctors get sick." I think these anxieties we are experiencing seem to be a somewhat ancestral. As if the human species is facing a transformation an evolutionary leap, as if we are experiencing new, unconscious ways of being. As if we have been suddenly immersed in a living "memory of the future", in a quantum temporal leap. These wandering thoughts are in search of a later reconnection. Later I watch TV and Recalcati is on La7 Channel, where he has the courage to give his usual sermons on "re-found brotherhood", and while preaching, he also begins advertising his non-profit organization "which has set-up a help desk for all health care workers." Some people have no limits, I think, as I get to feel a surge of implacable rage. Narcissism really has no borders and analysts are not immune to it, speaking of contagions.

Day twenty-five

I haven't used my car in about four weeks, I don't even go out to buy a newspaper or go shopping. My nice newsstand friend brings them to me and in the morning I find them in the mailbox. My general practitioner and my family have ordered me not to go out: I suffer from an immunodeficiency caused by Herpes Zoster, which is now chronic, caused by a previous bout of chickenpox that I contracted about ten years ago. Shortly before the epidemic, my general practitioner who has also been my friend for at least 30 years, had strongly advised me to investigate the state of my frail immune system with ad hoc tests. After having two attacks of ocular herpes with consequent corneal injury, various conjunctivitis, and very annoying recurrent shingles, he is convinced that the situation should be looked into. A few days ago he told me not to dare to leave the house. He is at his limit: he receives a hundred calls a day and is running out of masks. I wouldn't dare leave the house. I feel I'm surrounded by a lot of affectionate concern that on the one hand makes me happy and reassures me and on the other hand makes me truly understand, once again, how incredibly fragile we are, and I am. Then this morning a little spoof with my family was touching: against everyone's opinion I decide to go out and buy the newspaper, wearing my mask, of course. I feel like going for a walk, for God's sake, and of course I'm taking my self-certification! As soon as I'm dressed to go, and I reach the door, my wife and sons barge out of their rooms in combat gear. Sooner than you know it, I take off my jacket and retire to my chambers. Alessandro writes me a WhatsApp: "Daddy, we are not trying to make you unhappy, but we are doing it for you. We love you so much that we want to protect you." No, going out is unthinkable, I say to myself. I notice that even my patients ask me "How are you?" at the beginning of every session on Skype or WhatsApp. By now, it's become almost a ritual, a new element of the setting, which had never appeared on the scene before.

Day twenty-six

Today I am moved by my colleagues. This morning I read the email that one of them sent to me. He is a friend, as well as a colleague, and while I read his words, I can barely hold back my tears, something that rarely happens to me, in truth. He describes his experience in detail, as a true survivor of the Coronavirus contagion in March, his hospitalization in a sub-intensive therapy ward for a very serious Covid-19 pneumonia, the slow, precarious and tiring recovery from the illness, the contacts with his patients worried about his health, the unimaginable anxiety of his family, a dramatic experience. But now he is cured. His words intensely resound in me: we have many things in common, in addition to being part of the same psychoanalytic society. His words shake me up, I would like to answer him right away, but I feel the need to find an inner order in my emotional centre of gravity, a "permanent centre of gravity", like in Battiato's song, a centre of gravity that I think "is never permanent"; I wait before I answer him. I'd like to say many things to him, I need to "digest" his email, before sending him something that sounds "right" to me and even here I realize that I don't know what words to use. Then another Piedmontese colleague writes to me, almost verbatim: "I miss my daughters whom I haven't seen for a month. I miss my patients. I miss my colleagues. I miss my mountain." I try to spend the day reading the newspaper: I am struck by a beautiful article by Vittorio Lingiardi that talks about the "secondary trauma", that is, the fact that we are all experiencing a sort of collective, continuous post-traumatic stress disorder, especially the doctors and nurses, indeed those who I see every day on Skype – but the trauma leaves signs, which will come back later. Lingiardi writes: "The signs of the masks will fade from the faces of our doctors and nurses, but not from their psyche. Not right away, at least. Not all at once." I realize how much I agree with him. The problem is that the "sign of the masks" will remain in the psyche of each of us. And when we make it to the "after", which I imagine will be a long time coming after crossing this wasteland, each one of us, each therapist, will have to lift rubble and to heal wounds, including, first of all, their own. We will all have to rethink our internal emotional centres of gravity, we will have to, like the Jedi of Star Wars, fight to move away from and transform "the dark side of Force".

I dedicate the song "Permanent Center of Gravity" by Battiato to the colleague I was talking about at the beginning. I imagine him as being one of those "brave captains" the songwriter talks about.

Day twenty-seven

I can't believe I didn't hear any ambulance sirens today. Up until yesterday there were at least five or six ambulance sirens a day. I stopped counting them. Today everything is quieter, more peaceful. The only problem is that, for some mysterious reason, my computer ran an unrequested update, and now I can't access it anymore. Luckily, I have one of my sons who, being a computer scientist, is working on it to get the boat afloat again. Apparently, lately I've been pushing it into emotional storms and towards very dangerous reefs, and it's exhausted and wants to be left alone. Michele will be my Saviour, on this strange Palm Sunday, I know it for sure, with Salvini who keeps asking to keep the churches open at Easter. He is, as usual, a political parasite even in dramatic situations like these, using the religious sense of the Italian people for publicity, even when hundreds of his fellow citizens die in hospitals. In the meantime, I manage to write an email to my friend and colleague who has finally been resurrected after the difficult experience of hospitalization he had to undergo. I think I have found the right words to express my feeling of solidarity to him. Always in the "meantime" (but which "time", and which "between", I wonder while writing?), today I am living, together with all my fellow Lombards, the novelty of the Fontana decree that obliges us to go out only wearing masks.

I wore the mask when I took Dylan out in the middle of the fields. While I was walking in the grass, leaves and brushwood, I thought of an imaginary painter standing there among the trees painting a picture of me walking with Dylan at my side. And I was ironically thinking of the title of this post-surrealist work: Man Walking in the Country with Dog and Mask. Then I imagine the same scene, but in Banksy style, painted on a tall white building in the deserted city of Milan, that I miss, with its narrow streets, its chaotic traffic, its crowded bars and the Colonne di San Lorenzo full of young people with their beers, noisily celebrating their blossoming youth. I also miss Pavia, I can admit it: I haven't been on Corso Cavour, or to the Il Delfino bookshop, for more than a month, where I always spent time with my bookseller friends on Saturdays talking about Joe Lansdale, De Giovanni, William McIlvanney. Returning from this inner journey that was prompted in me by walking only five hundred metres in the countryside, Michele informs me that my pc has come to new life, under his miraculous computer hands. He worked on it all afternoon. "It was difficult, but I succeeded", he tells me smiling, with that wonderful, discreet and shy unique smile of his. Every now and then some good news. I recall Trilussa's poem, "A bee lands on a rosebud; drinks from it, and flies away ... All in all, happiness is a small thing". After all, these days happiness is not a "small thing". It's a time when you're content with very little. But the truth is, it's not a small thing.

Day twenty-eight

As I am about to write this page of my diary, I realize that we are on the 28th day of this tragic collective lock-down, of this macabre dance that involves us all. This "day 28" reminds me of the film *28 Days Later* by Danny Boyle, the director of *Trainspotting*. The film is beautiful, and once again demonstrates the unquestionable talent of this acclaimed director. It talks about how a dangerous virus is accidentally released from an English research laboratory and the infected people turn into vicious killers. A film about "zombies", which I highly recommend to my friend Luca Nicoli, who I think might like it (he has an understandably ambivalent relationship with horror). In 28 days the epidemic spreads and the survivors gather to flee from the city. Well, we can't escape from the city. In these days both I and my patients content ourselves with our dreams in which we frequent crowded places, conventions, theatres, premieres and vernissages where there is a lot of vitality circulating. I am struck by this oneiric affinity. Even a psychologist intern of mine, whom I see on Skype, tells me about dreams in which she goes to the pool with friends to have fun. However, the truth is another: these days when good news alternates with bad news. For example, a doctor patient of mine writes to me saying that he won't be able to be present at the session: a close relative of his wife, just 60 years old got worse and has unfortunately passed away. There will be no funeral, only two people can say a simple farewell, and he and his wife, who is also a doctor, cannot decide who will go. Another patient, who works in the forlorn areas of Bergamo for the ambulance dispatch, tells me that every night, when she goes home, she cries. She is very happy when the days of our session arrive, so that she can talk to me. I am also happy when I can talk to my colleagues, when I can try to dream collective dreams with them, like last night, when there were 25 of us on Zoom, all analysts of a clinical research group of the Centro Milanese di Psicoanalisi "Cesare Musatti". We talked about "holes of representability", the difficulty, the mental fatigue to fill these holes, the primary need to stay close to our patients, the idea of "presence", beyond the noble but now useless psycho-analytic concept of "interpretation". We talked about how the lockdown forced an adolescent patient to speak to her therapist by phone from the courtyard of the health facility where she is a resident, and how to make her feel present notwithstanding the distance. I'm reminded of Danny Boyle, his "28 days later". I've always thought, in line with Freud, that artists, directors, often manage to have prophetic glances of the future.

Day twenty-nine

Many thoughts, many reflections, many emails already written and many still to write. During all of this long day, I don't know why but I keep thinking about what I wrote in my book *On the Uncanny* – the difficult years that Freud lived through during the First World War. Very hard years, in which Freud wrote to Ernest Jones about the daily difficulties he encountered in his work, to keep his studio open, to carry on the "cause" of Psychoanalysis, his children at the front, the anger he felt when he couldn't find the wood to heat his studio. Of course, I have often reflected and written about these distant years. Years in which an oppressive sense of death hovered over Vienna and all of Europe. The years in which Freud wrote what was then entitled "*The Uncanny*", published in 1919, when (I didn't realize it until after its publication) my book came out in 2019, exactly 100 years later. Now we live another kind of Uncanny, I thought today, characterized, not by a war, that is, but by an event that can be defined and ritually standardized, that is known and experienced: there is "the enemy", there are the borders to defend, there are the partisans, but there is also the ceasefire, the truce. Now, the enemy has become a subtle bewilderment, an infiltrating melancholy that can be repre-sented only in certain TV series, like *The Leftovers* for example. Something that suddenly and radically changes our perspectives. And we still don't have a "traumatic theory" that can give structure to this change, and thus generate a mutual sense of awareness.

Day thirty

Sometimes the house seems like NASA's headquarters in Houston. Each of us is in their own room or in their study in front of a terminal: Alessandro in videoconference with Cairoli High School for distance learning; also my wife is either in the living room or the kitchen and teaching her young students; I myself, via Skype with patients and colleagues; Michele talks to his girlfriend and friends. From underneath the doors of every room you can hear an abrupt "Can you hear me?", "I'm connected", "I'm on the phone". Every once in a while, I expect someone to say the famous phrase, "Houston, we have a problem". But that this association with Ron Howard's 1995 film "*Apollo 13*" might not be just a coincidence. In fact, today, I'm also confronted with the fact that my wife will have to go back to the hospital and do several more tests. The contact with healthcare is becoming stressful, if not persecutory, because of my patients, the doctors, the nurses, my general practitioner, my Herpes Zoster, for now in silent retreat, and now my wife as well. The abruptness behind the doors of the rooms of our home reassures me a bit, it gives me a sense of vital flow, of "connection", of a bond that continues, despite everything, despite the sirens that I still hear from afar sometimes. Sometimes I do feel a bit as if I'm on Apollo 13 these days. I also feel like saying into the radio: "Houston, we have a problem".

Day thirty-one

We receive many phone calls and messages from friends, colleagues, and relatives asking about my wife's health. Many fond endearments of loving care from everyone. At home we also start talking about the Easter menu, which seems to be a good sign, also because my family is divided into two amusing factions: the vegetarian-macrobiotics (Ale and my wife) and the carnivorous-anthropocene (Michele and myself) – if I were to decide I would cook fettucce with wild boar ragout following a Tuscan recipe, and then I would go on to eggs with tuna, and then Easter "Colomba" and classic chocolate egg. The two vegetarians naturally look at me with disgust and counterattack with vegan lasagna and hazelnut crisp with melted chocolate and various grains with names that I can't even remember. Well, I think, the table will host an array of a wide variety of delicious foods, which maybe will lift our spirits a bit. Tomorrow I'm going to be on vacation. I made this decision, following the warm suggestion of a dear friend and colleague of mine from Milan, to clear my mind and give myself a break. I'm almost tempted to not work even on Tuesday, in line with the school holidays. In 30 years of work, I have hardly ever had any Easter holidays, only (long) summer and Christmas holidays, but this year is different, a year that turned out to be an increasingly steep climb during the first three months. In the mountains, you have to stop, after a long walk, sit down, and eat a chocolate bar. I somehow consider these days of "vacation" like this, they are necessary. So, I know, the steep climb will start again next week, hoping that the path will become flatter in some parts and can see some glades of temporary serenity.

Day thirty-two

ALE: "Are you writing a diary?"
I: "Yes."
ALE: "Like Anne Frank?"

Alessandro makes me smile and is very heart-warming. Our current quarantine reminds him of Anne Frank's condition as a recluse. He is the one who feels this way, because he misses his break dance, he misses his classmates, the school. Today he said to me as we went for a long walk in the countryside with Dylan: "Look at the beautiful sunshine, it would be the ideal day to go to the hills for a picnic". I was reminded of many other Easter picnics in Val Tidone, in the hills of Oltrepò Pavese, with our lifelong friends, with Dylan diving into the water of the stream. When I was little, we had a house there, I spent the whole summer there with my brother and my parents. It was a little house in a small village of less than one hundred inhabitants, full of children from various areas: some from Parma, some from Milan, some from Pavia. There were many children, and we all played together. They were adventurous, wonderful summers. Alessandro's "picnic" reminded me of those days when I felt a great sense of freedom, when we used to go to the meadows to pick wild strawberries between spring and summer, or blackberries, and we used to take them home and eat them with sugar all together in the courtyard of my house, while the cats were purring and rubbing against each other. There was a huge green field sloping down towards the old furnace near the Tidone riverbed that we could see from afar, a meadow surrounded by robust, tall chestnut trees, which seemed even taller in our children's eyes. There would be no picnic instead on this anomalous, lopsided Easter. I spent this day queuing – for the first time in a month in a small supermarket nearby, I wanted to try to see what the world had become. I thought it was a bit strange when they took my temperature at the entrance. "36.1°C: you can pass", the security guard told me. All wearing gloves and masks, weighing salad and zucchini, looking at the big Plexiglas barriers in front of the cashiers. I don't know why, but at the end of the day I was reminded of Nanni Moretti's "The son's room". Maybe it's not strange, since it talks about a psychoanalyst facing a serious loss. We all suffer from many losses. Too many deaths, too many illnesses. It was a melancholy first day of vacation.

Day thirty-three

Finally, today I organized a Skype meeting with Stefano and Luigi, my lifelong friends. Luigi in particular, had been my desk mate since middle school. It's still the same for me today, that is, I imagine our friendship as if we had been behind that desk since we were 11 years old. Now schools are closed, however, and so we are content with an aperitif on the terrace of my house.

Before that, I will dedicate myself to the duck ragout: I didn't find the boar unfortunately, but we'll make up for it nevertheless, in an uncertain tomorrow. I was reflecting this morning on this daily diary that I am writing in the intimacy of home and my study. I was thinking about the fact that usually, when I write a book for example (I've written three, two by myself and one with some colleagues in Milan), I imagine the process of writing as a one-man navigation, and at a certain point – let's say halfway through – I begin to "see the land", even if still far away. In these days writing my diary gives me a completely opposite feeling. I don't know where it will take me, I don't know when it will end, I don't see any land. The ship is rocking and the sea is big. Today, fortunately, the sea seems calm and flat. A strange calm, with the sun shining brightly. I think I'll close the Diary when I start seeing my patients in person again and not just virtually. But I don't know when that will happen. We are living the times of "not yet", another thought for reflection today. This is usually the time teenagers live in. It's very difficult, as teenagers know, to live the "not yet" time. After all, we are progressively turning into an adolescent society, navigating in its uncertain becoming, at the mercy of difficult uncontrollable "drives" and "developmental tasks". While waiting to "see the Promised Land", I wish everyone a Happy Easter.

Day thirty-four

This Easter we are celebrating resilience. Today, after lunch, we all sang "Bella Ciao" together, out on the terrace while I played Michele's electric guitar. I felt like I was in an episode of the series *The Paper House*. I could hear Berlin and the Professor, Nairobi and Tokyo, in the midst of my flowered hellebores, next to the ivy vases, caressing Dylan, while inspiring our singing. We kept talking about this theme of resistance all day long, as well as memories, of the discovering habits that had been set aside too hastily by the frenzy of our lives, prior to the epidemic. I pulled out my guitar, which I hadn't played for at least a year, and fished out my notebook with the many songs I had written since the nineties. I had interrupted that pleasurable hobby, because of being overcome by a thousand commitments, institutional and clinical responsibilities. Reopening the notebook, I noticed that many of the songs I wrote are love songs for my wife. And I started playing them in the living room, like I used to do at least 30 years ago, when we didn't have children yet, and in the evening, after a day's work in the psychiatric hospital, I relaxed playing my guitar, and writing lyrics and music. My wife was very moved, I wasn't expecting it, we were very moved together. It had really been years since I found the time to play my guitar, to dedicate myself to this old passion of mine left behind. It took the Coronavirus, I said to myself, to rediscover these emotions that seemed lost. I have always liked to sing, and write songs, since my university days, when I lived in Venice, and in the summer evenings, leaning on a windowsill of my house in Campo San Lorenzo, I wrote my first songs in ink on a notebook, duly in rhyme. And I always wrote them in rhyme, until the last ones, which date back to the 2000s, some dedicated to Michele, Alessandro, friends, as well as my wife. All this came from "Bella Ciao", a song of resistance, a song of passion for freedom and life.

I suggest everyone should watch this beautiful video, from *The House of Cards*, a TV series that I love – I guess you understood: https://www.youtube.com/watch?v=spCdFMnQ1Fk.

Day thirty-five

Last night as Dylan and I were on the last outing of the day, I suddenly noticed that the large garden of the residence where I live was completely untended and overgrown, including the lawns all around the complex. The gardeners haven't been here in a while and you can tell, in fact at one point I found myself crossing a flowerbed in the dark with grass up to my hips. Even Dylan was struggling hard to get through this unkempt jungle. I was looking out on desolate meadows, stretches of dandelions, unimaginable quantities of field daisies, it was no longer the garden with the perfect lawns, mowed with precision, leaving that distinctive scent of freshly cut grass that I love, and that I smelt as soon as the gardeners passed. I was reminded of the beginning of "The Waste Land" by T.S. Eliot, a poem written between 1921 and 1922, in Switzerland:

> April is the cruellest of months, breeding
> Lilacs out of dead land, mixing
> Memory and desire, stirring
> Dull roots with spring rain.

Yes, this April is cruel, in a moment that we are confronted by a self-inflicted desolation, we forget that we are part of Nature that we have never heeded, perhaps since the days Eliot wrote his poem. This virus violently tells us we must learn to put aside our omnipotence, our eternal human hubris. We were in an illusory bubble, I was pondering today, as I did last night as I strode through the tall, dishevelled grass in the garden, and I felt like Charlie Chaplin in the factory machine gear of *Modern Times*, only that we humans created that gear, I thought today. And in particular I am referring to predatory finance, weapons lobbies, the omnipotent proliferation of computer companies, the incredible velocity in moving goods, people and tourists: an excitatory and manic capitalist frenzy that has slowly corroded the foundations of the world like an acid. Our world is now "A Waste Land". And what's more, tomorrow and repeatedly for days, my wife must once again cross the threshold of a hospital, and stay there for hours, to undergo tests and visits. This year: "April is the cruellest of months" for me as well.

Day thirty-six

Today I start working again. I am oscillating between a sensation of subtle lethargy and a desire for vitality, movement and mental stimulation. On one hand, I feel a sense of torpidity, a craving desire for a long sleep full of variegated dreams where I always find myself in crowded places. I am plagued by an unexplainable fatigue at the end of the day, which alternates with feelings of incredible mental lucidity and vigour. I really hope that this last state of mind isn't the mental dimension that Meltzer defines as "delusion of clarity of insight", determined by an undoubtedly claustrophobic situation. In the meantime, my work proceeds. A patient emails me his "science fiction diary", set in a world inhabited by zombies. Instead, a young colleague in supervision sends me some sessions of a new case she wants to talk about on Wednesday afternoon. Other colleagues call me to share thoughts and reflections, others send me a review of a TV series to be published on Spiweb. I also find the time, between one patient and another, to write a review of the interesting English TV series *Broadchurch*. In short, a whole busy day full of various forms of written communication, all remote, at a distance calling me to notice the absence of the body, the bodiless nature of this moment we are living. Last but not least, along these lines, there are my hands today: I discover my hands are completely chapped by continuous washing, that has become almost an unconscious reflex that I do, after reading the newspaper, after picking up the mail, after picking up the pizzas that I bring home. My last patient of the day also tells me about her need for contact, warmth, closeness, which her boyfriend denies to her. And now, I acknowledge, so am I.

Day thirty-seven

ALE: "I'm going shopping, should I buy coffee? What kind?"
I: (thoughtfully): "The Covid coffee, we had it last time too."
ALE: "... what are you saying?! The coffee's called Covim."

My slip of the tongue persuades me that the virus has entered our unconscious. I said "Covid" instead of "Covim", I was really convinced that the coffee in the TV ad with the young Chinese girl saying "Buonissimo!" ("Yummy!") was called Covid. The fact is this, and it means that our unconscious has been perpetrated by the thought of the virus, its anguish, its semantic potential, not only biological–viral, with its perturbing ghostly nature. And it produces lapses. Like mine this morning. It's obvious, this is the only thing we speak about, all day long, everyday: the Covid-19 has imposed itself on our mind as a persecutory object that makes our most usual and natural PS-D oscillations rust, that tarnishes our contact barriers, that bends our alpha function. That's why we are more tired in the evening, although we are locked in the house from morning to night, apparently safe because we are reassured inside the protection of our four walls, of our household habits, of our daily rhythms. This familiarity, nevertheless, has its dark side, its extraneousness: the "heimliche" that becomes "unheimliche". We now yearn for an external reality, almost as if it were that which is more "familiar" and now lost that we long for, when before "external" coincided with "foreign". But, it is the reality inside us that is changing. That's where we should be looking. As my coffee incident was a clear reminder.

Day thirty-eight

Today went relatively well. In the morning, I had three sessions, that were very demanding and crowded with dreams, all of which were quite elaborate, vivid and very challenging, as if unconscious currents were looking for roads and karst paths where they could unfold their sense and desire to become. A "wish of becoming", Ogden would perhaps say. Dreams full of waterfalls, of water currents flowing through the audio speakers of my computer onto my couch, looking for openings, dikes, then settling in closures, riverbeds to generate new spaces of thought. After the three patients in the morning, I participate in a clinical group with some colleagues from Milan, which is reassuring because, it's like a familiar oasis of peace, where we usually talk about adolescent patients. In fact, a colleague talks about a new young patient with a first interview via Skype. The colleague is amazed, it is the first time in her life that she sees a teenager at a first consultation interview on a monitor, not in person, after meeting his parents, always online. We are happy to have a group which creates a holding environment where we can share our thoughts about these new, previously unthinkable, ways of clinical contact. The meetings with patients in the afternoon follow the placid trend of those in the morning, with my doctor patients who seem to me more serene, less stressed by the emergency. Once again, they speak of their dreams, visions, longings for open places, memories of distant people who live in Bali – and pagodas, and floaty, serene seas appear again. A very productive day, I say to myself, intense, full of concentration, "attention and interpretation". I water the plants between one patient and the other. It's relaxing. But then I get the news that Sepúlveda died. But then I think of water again, the plants need my attention, maybe because I begin to feel a bit bonsai, like a sort of Robinson Crusoe on my own island. It doesn't take me long to climb to the top to see its contours from above.

Day thirty-nine

This long day completely focused on the sessions, listening and thinking about how to maintain the "analytic function of the mind" alive where all our movements are altered by this forcibly limited situation. Today's "selected fact" was the fear of infecting parents. Practically all the patients, especially

Psychoanalytic diary in the lockdown   31

adolescents and late-adolescents, dwelt on their desire to get out, to resume their interrupted projects – university exams, internships, girlfriends they hadn't seen for more than a month, sports activities – but then also on the contiguous fear of "going home" and infecting their older parents. A patient, forced by the lockdown to live with his parents again just when he had recently moved away by moving to another city to study. He describes a "panic attack" that his mother has when he expresses the desire to go out as soon as the mythical "phase 2" begins. "Can you explain it better?" I ask him. His mother is distressed that he's going out and meeting friends, only to come home and infect her. I dismiss the various interpretations that emerge in my mind. But at the end of the day, I think about how this virus is affecting every generation. Some parents are afraid of their children: primitive Oedipal scenarios are reactivated, sons killing fathers. Or I listen to mothers – other patients – who are afraid for their teenage children's health, all of whom have come to their original homes after having moved away. Mothers who, as soon as their children have become independent, go back to being worried hens, trying to keep them under their protective wing. They illude themselves that they can protect them forever, as when they were in the womb, safe from any danger. I think this bitter period is somewhat quite tragic, also disrupting the thick texture of generations, which severs the idea of Future, as a precious mental object, as a container of our Self. A future that has become a horizon sliding down an inclined ramp that never seems to end, a scenario illuminated by oblique lights on a stage on where there will be the representation of a new, unpublished theatrical work by Samuel Beckett.

Day forty

Ale and I decide to make a movie. I think it's appropriate. A great way to start the weekend. You have to start with the script. I propose to start with a sound intro: the song "Una giornata al mare" by Paolo Conte, sung by Conte himself, and I make Ale listen to it, unexpectedly, he really likes it. I have two creative children, I tell myself, one composes music, the other dances: what more could I want? Now Ale has discovered this new hobby of making videos, so this seems to be the right occasion to try our hand at film-making. In fact he has just bought a wonderful video camera with Christmas tips he received from all our relatives. I've been writing for years, but I never wrote screenplays, they seem too difficult, too descriptive. "Exterior night. A deserted street, lit by streetlamps. No noise. Not a single car passes for at least two minutes of filming. Then handheld shots in the middle of the road for about a minute and a half." "Inside, daytime. A flashing alarm clock. The sound of the alarm clock. A hand comes out of the blankets and looks for it to turn it off. Three tries, no luck." We'd like to describe a typical day of lockdown. "But I also want to put some scenes where I dance", says Ale. "And I want to put in my studio with the couch", I say. I'm reminded of the film *La Pazza*

32 Angelo Antonio Moroni

Gioia by Paolo Virzì, one of the few recent Italian films, together with *Cuori Puri* by De Paolis, that I also liked. Besides "L'isola sbagliata" by my friend Giorgio Magarò, of course. Ale and I are having a great time, a "pazza gioia" (a crazy joy). I think, we need a dose of hypomania in this world that has suddenly become deserted.

Day forty-one

Entropy – I

These days, I have been reflecting on what type of psychoanalytic glance could be useful in interpreting what is happening to all of us, in our lives, in our minds. I was trying to find the meaning of the phenomenon as a whole, the transformations that are happening, inside and "outside" of us, how to grasp them, how to deal with them. The current pandemic is in fact an event that involves and overwhelms all the human domains known so far, somehow putting them all in even greater relation to each other. This is also "globalization". In this conjuncture, aspects of physical health are concretely related to those concerning emotions, relations and mental health. And these, in turn, cannot be separated from other areas such as economics and politics. Today's pandemic shows us, in short, that we have forgotten that each individual life depends on other people's lives. I think there are no particular meta-psychological concepts or psychoanalytic theories to use to examine such a complex problem. The word "entropy" came to my mind. It is a term used in Physics, not Psychoanalysis. Physics and Psychoanalysis, however, have much more in common than it seems. That is why I would like to dedicate a few pages of this diary to "entropy". First, however, a brief, modest premise on the relationship between Psychoanalysis and Philosophy of Science. Then I'll stop: I promise, and I'll move on to talk about entropy, which, then, seems to me to be a symbolically gravid term to effectively describe what has been happening for more than a month now. According to the Philosophy of Science, one of the major common objections to scientific realism is that it refers to semantic theses, that, attribute the reality of observed facts exclusively on the basis of the context of observation. The scientific paradigms with which human knowledge evolves (starting from the first infantile theories, up to quantum mechanics) are, however, undoubtedly the result of a psycho-affective travail that concerns both the individual and his group. However, even temporary, compliance with a given symbolic paradigm is nevertheless necessary for man, since it defends him from CHAOS. Cassirer has spoken at length about this, even when he writes: "Instead of the flowing content, the unit of a closed and hence permanent form predominates" (free translation of the author) (Cassirer, E., *Philosophy of Symbolic Forms*, Florence, La Nuova Italia, 1984). Man needs "closed forms" that defend him from chaos, but this also explains the attacks on this yearning for fulfilment. It is equally true that man is fascinated by chaos, because it frees him from the sense of finiteness. Moreover, excessive closure in symbolic forms does not produce knowledge, but inhibits the passage to successive paradigms. In this sense, as I said at the beginning, Psychoanalysis should perhaps gaze towards a new paradigm, but perhaps more in the realm of Physics rather than, strictly speaking, to Psychoanalysis, which involves the theme of ENTROPIA. Especially starting from this "catastrophic change" that we and our society are experiencing.

Day forty-two

Entropy – 2

> What we don't see affects our lives more than we think.
> (Tokyo, *The Paper House*, Season 4, Episode 4)

Entropy in Physics measures the disorder in any kind of physical system. To better explain we can say that the entropy of a system increases when it passes from a state of ordered equilibrium to a disordered one. The entropy rate also provides information about the direction in which the system evolves and is transforming itself. The concept of entropy is related to Chaos Theory, which relates the entropic, disordered state of a system to its so-called "sensitive dependence on initial conditions". This dependence signals the fact that, in a chaotic system, even very small variations in the initial conditions can correspond to considerable variations in the future behaviour of the system. We are talking about the so-called "butterfly effect", introduced by the mathematician Edward Lorenz in 1972, in his well-known article "Predictability: Does the flapping of a butterfly's wings in Brazil cause a tornado in Texas?" This is a metaphorical title, of course, but it describes what can be analysed through real mathematical models. A consequence of the sensitivity of a system's evolution to initial conditions is that if we have little information about the system's initial entropic state, then the future of the system will not be predictable beyond a certain time. We are well aware of this, when considering weather forecasts, which cannot go beyond a certain number of days. Even the unconscious, after all, works as a continuously expanding entropic system of relations and emotions, and that's why I think that meteorological metaphors can be used in attempting to represent it. Psychoanalysis is in fact a sort of hot-air balloon journey. A hot-air balloon can only go up and down, it has limited movements, but when it goes up you obtain a wider perspective. Going up, it is then transported by the winds of transference and countertransference, but we cannot predict how these interactions will develop. Above all, we cannot direct its movement. Psychoanalysis, like hot-air balloon trips, takes place in unpredictable weather-like unconscious conditions. "What we don't see affects our lives more than we think", as Tokyo says in *The Paper House*. You have to trust the pilot, who, in addition to his expertise, also puts passion into his work, which is the fire that inflates the balloon. But the entropy in the system can increase immeasurably and the poor balloon has to resist against the difficult meteorological phenomena – both the external ones and those that move the unconscious. That's what's happening these days. Psychoanalysis has tried to describe what I have called "entropy" in many ways. But I'll come back to it tomorrow.

Day forty-three

The idea of "entropy" in psychoanalysis can be considered from various theoretical points of view. First of all, in psychoanalysis, the cause of disorder in a psychic system where its narcissistic homeostasis is disrupted, that is its (always illusory) *ubi consistam*, has always been defined with the term TRAUMA. Trauma is, therefore, a frustrating experience, because it forces us to abandon previous theories, modes and ways of being to adapt to the unknown. Reality (internal and external) is always unknown, it is always chaotic, reality is interaction, co-creation of meaning. In psychoanalysis, the failure of the "traumatic theory" of hysteria is sufficient to show, to see how this trauma forced the first psychoanalysts to go from the suggestive to psychoanalytic technique. But this also led to the discovery of the new concepts of "countertransference", "projective identification" (M. Klein), "PS-D oscillation" (Bion), "transitional object" (Winnicott), "transformative object" (Bollas) and so on. Another theory that can help understand the meaning of the term entropy in psychoanalysis is that of "repetition compulsion". The maximum of positive entropy, i.e. the tendency towards a zero degree of thermodynamic exchanges, tends in fact to fixity, i.e. death. Repetition compulsion tends to block emotional transformations, to crystallize them in a loop that rusts the mental apparatus. Identity is, in reality, a continuous oscillation between identity itself and the relative entropy of the subject, tension between remaining oneself and yearning to learn from experiences that transforms oneself into another = equal + n. Another psychoanalytic theory useful in the interpretation of entropy is that of the "death drive", a purely speculative idea introduced by Freud in 1921 in his work "Beyond the Pleasure Principle". At the basis of the compulsion to repeat, Freud places the death drive: the body's tendency to an absolute positive entropy, i.e. to death, to a so to speak a mineral state. It is opposed by Eros, the life drive, which continually tries to "bind" this contrary drive. I conclude with an ulterior theory, the one that introduces the Bionic concept of "beta elements". In Bion's theory of the growth of thought, the beta elements are the original constituents of what will later be thoughts. They are defined as "the sensory impressions of emotional experiences", i.e. any emotional and sensory movement that arises in the subject when he is in contact with external and internal reality, during sleep as well as while awake. Beta elements must pass through the alpha function to obtain knowledge of reality and successively implement an adaptive attitude towards it. The alpha function metabolizes the beta elements thus, transforming them into alpha elements, i.e. mental elements capable of representing and symbolizing reality. This way, a reality that otherwise would only be traumatic becomes mentally manageable. Beta elements present themselves as "undigested facts", as meaningless experiences. They are compared by Bion to the Kantian "thing in itself", to the "noumen" (which Bion calls O), unable to "bind" to each other to form images and representations of the state of things inherent to the external or internal world. Their course is purely entropic, chaotic. They are "facts" that are only destined to be evacuated, through acting out, that are supported by projective identification. Unlike their corresponding "metabolized" elements (the alpha elements), in fact, they are not able to bind together to form the structure of the mental apparatus called "contact barrier". This barrier is indispensable for preventing the unconscious interference in the conscious. Such interference would generate chaos, disorder. The beta elements therefore do not permit individuals to experience reality as a "phenomenon", in the Kantian sense, but as a "noumenon", where things have the meaning of words and words the meaning of things, typical of the experience of psychosis. Given their inability to "bind", these raw experiences are agglomerated in the psyche, forming the "beta screen", which has the function of evacuating the beta elements.

Day forty-four

For various reasons, I had to go to Milan this morning. Milan was full of sunshine but there were no people. A metaphysical experience. I felt like Dylan Dog, the famous comic-strip "para-normal investigator" on the go with a new adventure of his own. Meanwhile, driving with my mask on the Pavia freeway, my glasses kept fogging up. Then, astonished, I see new rice fields, probably flooded by farmers these days. I remember one my old songs, about rice fields at sunset. When I arrive downtown, I change my mask and put on an FFP2: much more comfortable, I realize that I can breathe better with this mask than with the surgical one, I don't know why, but it's true. My glasses don't fog up anymore. It's April but it feels like mid-August, with only a few rare cars every five minutes. Viale Liguria is a desert, all closed, without a soul in site. The trees in the avenue are green, like those in Piazza Risorgimento, but remote and immobile, suspended like in a painting by Magritte. I feel as if I have landed on another planet. I see one tiny greengrocer's shop that is open and I feel like photographing it, as if it were the last specimen of a rare type of orchid, now in danger of extinction on the planet Covid-19. Meanwhile the FFP2 mask gives off an annoying plastic smell, but it makes me breathe properly, so I put up with it. My patrol advances: all I see is an Indian street vendor selling lighters and other useless little trinkets, sitting on the floor, on the corner of Corso Indipendenza. Not a living soul for at least a mile. But under today's wonderful sun even Milan seems beautiful to me: this

Milanese "journey" seems to me like a holiday in the Galapagos, after almost 50 days of seclusion. The wooden trams are scarce and they look like sea turtles diving into the clear water of this limpid and dreamy day.

Day forty-five

Today I meet up with a lot of suffering. A doctor patient tells me, discouraged: "I mean, I think we're not going to get rid of this coronavirus any time soon." Three of his close relatives have passed away in the last two weeks because of the virus. A nurse, a friend of his is home sick. She used to work in a rest home. It is very painful for me to share these mournful emotions with a person who spends every day hospitalizing, treating and then, also, discharging patients and then returning to her family to bury her loved ones. One of the last deceased relatives wasn't even in his forties. I feel lost, at times, as if I were in exile, while I listen to this suffering that is seeking to be mitigated by tenderness. I think that several analyses in this period have gradually turned into treatments of "current neurosis", of current traumas, as in war, really. With some of my patients who are healthcare workers, in various branches, who are still at the front. Before now we didn't talk about deaths, comorbidities, "delirium" induced by neurological complications of the virus. We used not to talk, only, of such concrete, anatomical "things" like the sense of abjection of a cumbersome, declining body. Now, it happens. And so frequently that it is upsetting. And we are only a few days away from the reopening, the famous 4th of May that everyone is invoking as the "day of liberation". In the remote sessions we also talk about responsibility, "of who is to blame", of those who have killed to date more than 7,000 elderly people in Lombard retirement homes. Then this morning I read in the newspaper La *Provincia Pavese* that "rigid inspections of the ATS" (Agenzia di Tutela della Salute) have started. Reading it captures a motor of revolutionary, Bolshevik rage.

Day forty-six

It was a pretty quiet day. I contact several colleagues via email and on WhatsApp. We talk about scientific issues, but also about more pragmatic things, regarding our queries on what this blessed "reopening" in steps will be like, at least here in Lombardy: 4 May – 11 May – 18 May. We all agree that we should be very careful about seeing patients in our offices immediately. And I communicate the same caution to my patients during the remote sessions. The session with a young student is totally focused on the various types of mask, surgical, FFP2, NK95, anti-particulate, filter, NCN MR2, and so on. Unfortunately, I think to myself that, I'm learning a lot more about healthcare than I was interested in. My doctor patients tell me everything, symptoms, which parts of the body are affected by the viral infection, its course, with an abundance of details. Sometimes, it seems almost sadistic, I think. How do you move inside such a mass of "betalomas" (a term coined by Antonino Ferro) when you are immersed in a session? *Nachträglichkeit*, I think, posteriority: we will only learn by living. The young student says "After all, living is risky", and I can only agree with him. Did we forget? It seems so. He also tells me that he really thinks we are experiencing an epochal change that our posterity will read about in history books. As he speaks, I think back to a pre-adolescent fantasy of mine, which is the idea, almost a wish, indeed, that aliens would descend to earth. A desire combined with anguish, albeit, of the unknown. I think it was an idea linked to my own abandonment anxiety: "Are we alone in the universe? Is there no One else?" What would these aliens be like if we could actually meet them? In Spielberg's *The War of the Worlds*, based on the novel by H.G. Wells, these "aliens" aren't that good. I think this "alien" is not so good either even though it that comes from our earth and not from outer space. The young student greets me, because the session is over.

Day forty-seven

I go to visit my friends in Pavia to get some PPE (Protective Equipment) that I need and that they can get easily. Once again driving my car on the empty, desolate Pavia freeway seems extremely strange, especially, under the rays of the warm, placid sun. It seems like an oneiric Shyamalan film, with oblique, disorienting shots. Since the beginning of March, I haven't seen the Naviglio Pavese, the tree-lined avenue leading to the Pavia stadium, and the rotunda with the magnificent statues by Gio Pomodoro. The city, which has always been so familiar to me, is now an emotional blur, a source of melancholy sadness making me feel estranged and remote. I'm happy when I finally get to my friends' house, who naturally receive me in the condominium courtyard, with masks and obviously at a safe distance. I stop to talk with one of them on the concrete bench in the courtyard. It just doesn't seem real that I am meeting in person with a live human being who is not a member of my family. An elderly neighbour greets us, "The bench is clean, I disinfected it this morning, don't worry!", the woman reassures us, and we express our heartfelt gratitude. Another human being: fantastic! Then I decide to lie down in the sun, on the gravel in the courtyard, chatting with my lifelong friend, and I feel like I'm being extremely transgressive. We talk for a long time and my friend's words give me a sense of continuity. It feels so good to be there that I imagine I'm on a beach by the sea as I touch the pebbles, with that beautiful warm sun that reassures me. We feel deprived, I think – we are living an experience of deep deprivation: the pebbles of the gravel courtyard of the condominium make me "hallucinate" a beach, the sea, a climate of summer vacation. All of this on a Saturday that is then also 25 April, which I celebrated in streaming on the Repubblica website, listening to the Mameli's hymn sung by the choir of the Teatro San Carlo in Naples. All this has an oppressive, depressing, reflective feel. Then I virtually embrace my friend and I go home: same deserted streets, same sun, that Montale sun, the "hawk's ascent".

Day forty-eight

Another day dedicated to the sun. I want to stay outdoors with Dylan as much as possible, in the countryside, along the irrigation canals, listening to the restful gurgling of the water flowing out of the locks. Behind the house, large canals flow merrily along lined by poplars and happy oaks. I've always loved hearing the rustling of leaves in the midst of silence. When Michele was little, I used to take him on my bicycle seat, ride in the countryside and let him listen to the rustling of the leaves: I imagine that could be why today, at 20 years old, he loves listening to music so much. It's nice to walk in the sun with Dylan running far and wide. I start having very pleasant human encounters: for example, Roberto and Claudia, our nice neighbours with their female cocker-terrier, very friendly with Dylan. I think about how this canine and human multi-ethnicity that you meet outside is pleasant and vital. We proceed on the path in single file, naturally at safe distances and with our masks on, but we can chat and make invitations for coffee and, in a still indefinite future, to have a coffee together. We can wish for future encounters and wish for a future. Another thing that relaxes me a lot today, together with my wife, is to put away the many books scattered around the study and the house, many issues of the *Journal of Psychoanalysis*, many volumes that I no longer remember having. I am looking for my cherished *Greek Grammar* by Pieraccioni, which is still missing, and this sets off a debate on the use of the optative in ancient Greek language while we are having lunch. Alessandro is very interested in the subject and is surprised that there is a similar verbal mode, which does not exist in Italian. A mode that expresses intentionality, I think, once again desire, future. An intentional future, precisely, towards which one tends, which has not yet appeared. The Greeks had the sense of a becoming within a "panta rei" that flows like the water of the canals around my house. But I feel that we would also like to reconstruct this "becoming" which seems to have stopped, but that I can see still clearly in the eyes of my two sons, who talk to me about projects, ideas, music to write, constructions, tests to study for, work to do, books to write. Today is the day of "panta rei".

Day forty-nine

Another adventure for my wife in the hospital. Of course, I can't accompany her, they won't let me in, it's obviously forbidden. It's not easy for me to work thinking she's locked in a hospital, for hours, doing tests. Italian healthcare is becoming a bit persecutory for me these days and to think that I've been dealing with it for 30 years, as a healthcare worker. I have always linked with the places where I have worked in all these years: for example, a very large psychiatric hospital; at the entrance it had a very large fountain with goldfish which is still today an indelible and intense memory for me. Then, there are also the psychiatric communities, counselling centres for adolescents, communities for minors, public mental health centres, centres for autistic patients in developmental age. And then my private practice, of course. I feel like I have left behind something positive in all these places, may it be a contribution, an imprint, a new idea. My encounters and relations with the colleagues I met were also quite positive, and most of them are still very dear friends of mine. Some still work in the Public Service, others have preferred, like me, to do private activity and consultations. We have shared training and long days working with patients of all kinds, of all ages, except for children. I have never had the chance to take care of children. But I have worked with pre-adolescents and adolescents: generations of adolescents. Now, this Lombard Healthcare System, on the other hand, is putting me to the test, excluding me, keeping me out of the door; it worries me, I hear its cry of pain, through the stories of my patients, doctors, psychologists, child neuropsychiatrists, who lie down on my couch and transmit their suffering to me. And that's not enough – now I cannot see my wife either, she's kept away from my gaze, barricaded in a "clean" ward, precisely because it's severely off-limits to anyone but patients and staff.

Day fifty

Today's "selected fact" is corporeality. I am quite struck by the fact that the new Decree by President Conte, on the "reopening" of 4th May, seems to have deeply evoked the desire to see me in person, in almost all the patients I have spoken to today. All the free associations seem to converge on that point and on one question: "What do you think of the new Decree of 4th May regarding visiting relatives?" I feel a sort of "illogical joy", as Giorgio Gaber would say, in the patients' words. Phrases like: "Well, but we'll see each other later, won't we?", or "If we can see our relatives, then we can see each other again", and so on. In transference, patients and their analysts can be considered relatives as well, I think, exactly in the affective–emotional sense of the "constant conjunction". To say it with Bion, a conjunction creates a human bond between care-giver and patient in time following the rhythmic flow of the sessions and now has been disjointed suddenly and unexpectedly by "force majeure". A patient tells me that she can't wait to see her parents again, who she hasn't seen for a month. It seems to her that hugging them seems to be more important than "seeing them": "I see them every day on Skype". It is the desire for physical tactile contact, touching, feeling another person's body, the flesh and bones, which emerges as what I would define to be an archaic need. It is a need in which the here and now echoes its call to a lost holding, to a physical feeling. What does the child need? To feel the hardness of the humerus and forearm of the mother who supports him, who is there, and who makes the baby feel that she is entirely dedicated to him with her mind and with her love. I also feel as if I'm in a nursery these days, but I'm behind the glass, impeded from "holding the baby". A patient freely associates and says she feels as if she were inside a glass jar, like the peppers her grandmother put in brine when she was little. Just like my patients, I also feel the need to rehabilitate my humerus, and my forearm to resume their proper functioning.

Day fifty-one

All of today seemed to be a regressive jump into a childhood "psychic retreat". Almost all the patients were adolescents: a lot of them tell me about the Disney cartoons they have rediscovered in these days. *The Little Mermaid*, *Peter Pan*, *Mary Poppins*, *Cinderella* parade in front of me, vis-à-vis me on Skype, or, always on Skype, they all flow in from the earphones I use with my PC on the couch. Then there is the parade of teddy bears, soft toys, souvenirs bought in Paris, Prague, Stockholm, when they were little, all kept in old boxes in the basement, and resurrected, like Danny's talking toys in the movie *Toy Story*. Of course, then they also recall the parties with friends, discos, aperitifs, the "nightlife" in Piazza della Vittoria or the school break, the coffee machines, the nice janitor. But … But then I hear the sound of what is gone or what is lost: the dolls, the stuffed walrus "that my grandmother gave me", the memories "of when I went to the beach and my dad let me dive into the water from his back". All mixed with the fear of what "it will be like when I'll have to get in the car to go to university?" Then there are those who talk to me about rabbits, dogs, cats, all searching for a state of transition to assimilate a difficult, constricting reality that also keeps me far from those I see over there, behind the screen, who look at me and tell me their memories and their dreams. Regression? Social withdrawal in adolescence? Maybe, instead, I think it is the need for sharing, intimacy, of "row C", of learning how to deal with the fear of not being able to face the world again, and, like Peter Pan, finding the window of the house closed when he wants to go back in. In fact, Peter Pan comes to mind when I listen to another patient talking to me about Disney cartoons for the whole session.

Day fifty-two

This diary itself is developing a transitional function for me. It's a daily appointment that I feel I can't miss. I think it's an appointment with myself to keep my self-analytic function alive as well as my dreaming ability, my negative ability, call it whatever you want. Call me Ishmael, I feel like saying, to paraphrase Melville, as we sail together in this vast, open sea, with a hazy horizon, but there is no hovering dense static mist above us. The refractive dystopia of the sea makes me understand that Ithaca is still far away. There are no sirens in this sea so I don't have to tie myself to the mast to avoid being lured by their song. A silent, internal, deep sea. In the afternoon, in a short rest break between one patient and another, I dreamt I was in a new house, in a foreign country, in a large, very modern kitchen, and I saw a blond boy next to me, who in the dream was my new son. I took him in my arms and he smiled happily, and then we walked around the house together; I showed him various objects, prints, paintings, and at a certain point I saw him on the threshold of a grass door, as if it had just been cut, mixed with water. Here I said to the child: "See, here we also have a garden", and I thought to myself: "Here the water has also broken". In the following free associations, I imagined that the child was somehow my analytic function that my unconscious was telling me to take care of, because this is the only way I can act as a midwife. Like most psychoanalysts we try to help give birth to new thoughts, openings, new indoor/outdoor spaces, and new gardens where a possible shared sense can sprout.

Day fifty-three

Today I think of the providential Manzonian rain. I go out with Ale and Dylan in the country and we are surprised by a memorable downpour. Boots, umbrellas and a green raincoat for Dylan are practically useless and, in no time at all, we are completely soaked. Ale and I start laughing, as we have never laughed before. How nice to be together, we seem to be saying to each other. I don't know why but this purifying rain suddenly reminds me of a series of phrases in Pavia dialect. So, we start speaking in dialect, or rather Ale tries: he doesn't know this language very well, we don't speak it much at home. But I do know the Pavia dialect very well. Probably this contact with nature, these unpredictable weather events, or something that has come out of my preconscious, stir up these atavistic memories of a language spoken by my mother and that she taught me. A peasant language rekindled by the clods of earth from the ploughed fields, and which I unconsciously wish to pass on to my offspring. "Varda ti sa gh'é da mett sü i strivai pr'va a purtá föra âl cân, ades ca suma in dâl mes âd mag. Che temp lúc: piöva ca Diu la mândâ",[2] or "Chi a San Martin al par al Dilüvi Üniversal. Am par da ves Nué. Äm manca dumá l'arca".[3] And so now Ale and I are dying of laughter, with Dylan constantly shaking himself off as the torrential rain pours down into the canals that could overflow at any moment. I have a lot of fun with Ale in the country, I love being with him. I also love being with Michele, like that time we went to Copenhagen together, and then to Lund, Sweden. I love my children, I think to myself, in the middle of the pouring rain which is actually lots of fun for me today. Then, Ale and I go home and continue shooting our new short film, screenplay at hand. We study the shots, discuss the sequences, try to involve Michele in the casting, but he withdraws into his chambers. Today I don't feel like doing anything intellectual or professional. I just send my review of Leigh Whannell's *The Invisible Man* to Spiweb, and I watch the film again with Ale, who loves these types of thrillers. Then I reread the beautiful, moving diary of my friend Roberto Goisis, psychoanalyst, on Friday of the Republic today. It was an excellent 1st May. Two things to remember.

Day fifty-four

In 54 days now, this is only the second time that, driven by insane but human hubris, I have ventured out into the dangerous depths of a shopping mall and go into a supermarket. I'm faced with a long queue of Martians wearing masks of all colours: I have the fantasy of being Ian Solo when he enters Jabba the Hutt's lair in *Star Wars*. Shortly earlier, however, I felt a surge of childish happiness, just because I could drive my car again to go to the greengrocer. A sense of renewed vigour came over me when I held the steering wheel! I suddenly had a fantastic idea: I could leave and go to Genoa, or to the hills! It's not true, of course, but at least let me dream a little, I say to myself: I see the hills on the horizon, it's finally a clear day still bathed by a nice warm sun. As my hands grasp the steering wheel, swathed in my latex gloves, I feel an unsurmountable desire to go to Oltrepò Hills, find a remote and silent corner to lie down on a green meadow for hours and just look at the mass of scattered clouds, the vivid cirrus streaking the sky, the frayed solitary cloudlets all like handkerchiefs thrown in a bucket of blue water. I could really go, I tell myself, behind the wheel, and this suffices my need to evade for this morning. I find the usual queue at the greengrocer's, but time passes quickly as I speak on the phone with my dear friend Stefano, who I really love talking to. And above all he is my tennis partner, and every Sunday we happily run back and forth on the tennis field between a forehand and a backhand.

It's quite different at the supermarket. I wish I had Chewbacca next to me. I'm not Ian Solo. I'm alone. The line is endless. My friends' faces are quickly parading past me quickly in my mind, I wish I could see them in person ... I don't know how they are ... I really have to call them. All these thoughts race through my head like a whirlwind. Then, instead, I look around myself and everything seems terribly slow, but I finally arrive at the entrance of the supermarket, where they try my body temperature: 36.1C°. Good, I can go in. I am lost, it takes me about half an hour to find the curry, another half hour to find the coconut milk, that Ale wants to make an apple pie. Once again, I recall the bar full of aliens that Harrison Ford waltzes into, alias Ian Solo. The cashier seems to be most alien of all to me, she's dressed as a subintensive therapy doctor: she's wearing a mask, a double set of gloves, and has a plastic visor covering her face. "I wonder how hot it's going to get in there", I tell her. "Yeah, and then you think we'll have to work longer shifts to avoid crowds from forming. I'm sick of it." I understand, I feel sorry for her, and I think back to the stories of my doctor patients when they tell me about the careful, long, torturous dressing protocol before entering a Covid-19 ward. I'm also starting to get hot, only wearing a mask and one pair of gloves. I wonder what we'll do when it starts to get really hot, I wonder. Summer is not so far away. I go out, and in the parking lot, I drive my cart towards my Millennium Falcon.

Day fifty-five

Although I try to move as much as possible taking many long walks with Dylan out into the country, it seems like my muscles need more. By evening, my ankles and calves are sore and begging for tennis. I feel like I'm on an airplane, on a long transoceanic journey but I never arrive because the destination is too far away. Usually, during these long trips my ankles swell up and hurt. So, I have to try to stand and walk as much as possible along the corridor, taking off my shoes as soon as possible. It has always happened to me, because my peripheral vascular system is sensitive to high altitudes. Years ago, I was on Easter Island, a seven-hour flight from Santiago de Chile, and I still perfectly remember how tormented my poor ankles were. I am suffering from the same problem in these days which is strange and worrying for me. I often lie down on the living room carpet and do stretching my legs to help my leg muscles. This long period is really putting us to the test, making us suffer in body and spirit. It really seems to be like a new Uncanny, which reminds me of certain novels by Jeff VanderMeer, for example the *Area X Trilogy*, a fantastic river novel that I love very much. Two meetings today make me think, in my personal Area X: on my way back from my afternoon walk with Dylan, I meet an old lady who lives alone not far from me. Usually, she is very lucid and kind, while today she isn't even wearing a mask, and she tells me that she is afraid that there are strangers in the closet spying on her. I ask her if she is going shopping, and she says no, it, doesn't matter, she can skip meals anyway. I spend some time with her to try to understand if something is wrong with her (clinically) and finally I ask her for her son's telephone number, to let him know that his mother is not very well and needs help. Then, soon after, I meet my neighbour on the stairs. He is an architect with two small children. He has a long, unshaven beard, red tired eyes. It's the first time I've seen him so worn out, he's usually extremely well-kept and groomed, almost obsessively, at least according to my standards. I ask him how he is and he tells me that he's beginning to feel "tensions" in the family, they're all nervous. There's a tired and unusual tone in his voice. I tell him that if he needs us, we're there, just a stone's throw away. I'm upset by these encounters today, they make me perceive the strong emotional transformations that this forced cloister is making us go through, how our thought processes are undergoing complicated modifications. This era could inspire VanderMeer to write a new episode of his literary epic. We are all rolled into Area X.

Day fifty-six

I have no intention of adhering to the so-called "Phase 2", let alone reopening my study immediately. All the information I receive, from patients, relatives, infected and sick colleagues who have spent weeks in sub-intensive therapy, etc., etc., reinforce this decision of mine, of which I am becoming more and more convinced. As my friend and colleague Roberto Goisis writes and wisely states in some interviews he released after surviving Covid-19: this virus is an "ugly beast" that, if it can, assails us like an invisible alien, like those of VanderMeer's "Area X". On the other hand, I was wondering, how can you work with a patient in the studio if you feel anxious about getting sick? Or infecting someone? Or being infected? I don't agree at all with some colleagues that are convinced that analytic "neutrality" is completely at stake using the remote means of work. But, I say, isn't using Skype less damaging than working in person with anxiety to the so-called concept of "neutrality?" (one of many concepts that I consider to be obsolete together with other psychoanalytic armamentarium). Up until June, my studio will be closed.

Day fifty-seven

Today my patients made many free associations regarding recluse locations – distant, unreachable, sparsely populated hill trails. Landscapes of solitary life, which remind me of the poetics of Montale, of the "wall topped with sharp shards of a bottle", of a sea that you can only hear but cannot see. We are precluded of our analytic relationship. Other patients tell me about dogs that get lost in the mountains, that they find half-starved. Fortunately, the owner's phone number was on the collar and they were brought home. "Dogs that haven't eaten for days must be re-fed gradually, otherwise they could die", says a patient, who has been stuck at home for two months with her two children. She would at least like to resume her exercise routine at Vernavola Park, "but it won't be like before". The restrictions on relatives seem bizarre to us. "Psychoanalysis is also a significant emotional relationship", another patient tells me, "and who decides which relatives you can visit?". I certainly can't blame this patient and so we talk about needs, their subjective and personal nature, and how improbable that an impersonal government decree can grasp these subtle nuances. All these issues emerging in the sessions make me recall the psychosocial concept of "institutional syndrome", that is the combination of disabilities or deficits that develop after a person has spent a lot of time in a constrictive institution, for example a psychiatric hospital or a prison. Institutionalized people can be deprived of their freedom and sense of responsibility, to the point that once they leave the institution and return "to life", they find it very difficult to get used to normal rhythms of life again. If I remember correctly, Russell Barton first mentioned it in 1959 in his book *Institutional Neurosis*, and then the sociologist Erving Goffman. We also feel like those "dogs lost in the mountains that need to be gradually re-fed", described by one of my patients in their free association.

Day fifty-eight

I have to go to my general practitioner and friend, whose office is about 20 kilometres from my house to pick up some prescriptions for my wife. The studio is located in a small village in the Po Valley, and is usually surrounded by rice fields beginning from the month of May. I used to live there many years ago. And at that time, I left every morning to go to the Fatebenefratelli Psychiatric Hospital where I worked for many years. My GP and I remained friends; even after I moved to Pavia, I didn't feel like changing my GP and substituting him with a doctor closer to home. Going back to those places is always pleasant for me. Even this morning. It is also pleasant because they are close to where my mother and my maternal grandmother were born, who with her family had a mill where they ground wheat to make flour. My grandmother, with my great-uncle Alfredo, used to get on the cart with the horses, loaded with sacks of flour and distribute them in the various farms nearby. Once again, this morning, the Po Valley seems beautiful, bathed under a sun so hot that it is pleasantly surprising and makes me feel a slight sensation of relief, as if slightly lightening the heavy load of suffering created by this heavy lockdown we are enduring. An "unbearable lightness of being", I think, and I recall Milan Kundera, an author who takes me back during my University years to the Faculty of Psychology, when I begin to make new projects for my future. I see the general practitioner in the courtyard of the Town Hall, where he has his practice, wearing a mask, and this image brings me back to the present, from that "search for lost time" that was looming in my mind during the car trip on the roads of the Po Valley. There are other people waiting for him, and he is on the phone. He's tired, full of adrenaline, and very busy. He tells me that I can't enter the studio and that he'll pass the prescriptions through the door. I'm sorry I can't stop to have a chat with him and ask him how he is doing during this terrible moment in history we are all sharing. I feel consoled when I get back in my car and see the fields, the roundabouts, the petrol stations that parade along the provincial road. I feel like I've been on holiday abroad, only after driving just 20 minutes.

Day fifty-nine

These days, besides the requests I receive from people contacting for the Psychoanalytic Listening Group for the SPI Coronavirus Emergency Team, of which I am part, I'm getting phone calls from new patients asking me to start therapy and consultations via Skype. This worries me, since it somehow confirms a hypothesis of mine, which I would rather refute. The hypothesis is that the more we go on, the more we run into the effects of what the English psychoanalyst Masud Khan, in 1991, defined as "cumulative trauma": an infiltrative, silent, but continuous deposit of psychic micro-lesions that accumulate in our Self, embrittling it, until suddenly and, without any particular warning, it begins to become critically destabilized. The prevailing motivations of these new requests for therapy? "A feeling of oppression", "Anxiety that I have never felt before", "Panic attacks that I had when I was very young, never had since, that now have come back". I have the impression that a set of karstic, fluctuating, unconscious movements are coming to the surface, and will continue to surface more and more, as if this traumatic social phenomenon, like a sudden inflammation that touches us all closely, re-traumatizes once-sunken areas that now re-emerge and return to the light, wreckage that washed onto our beaches. Maybe that's why tonight, after all day working my studio, I was reminded of films that I would like to see again, like *The Bay* (2012) by the great Barry Levinson, or the brand new *Sea Fever* (2019) by Neasa Hardiman, which all focus on the theme of contagion. Almost prophetic, I would say.

Day sixty

Two months of paralysis is a long time. "Paralysis" is the word that came to my mind this morning, a very peculiar, bizarre paralysis in which many things happened anyway. Two months seemed like a whole year to me; we perceived time to have been somehow dilated undergoing several inclinations, distortions and deformations. I continued to work, perhaps more than before: sessions, new patients, writing papers and reviews, drafting a very ponderous book with a group of colleagues from Milan and I am the general editor. I finished two other books on adolescence which I am proposing to publishers, invitations to present my book in some Italian cities, film reviews and several psychoanalyses suspended and to be reorganized. I am organizing many vital, creative projects, inside myself and outside myself, but there everything is constantly influenced by this burdening sense of paralysis. Not to mention the summer holidays. Towards the end of February, I was already dreaming of a relaxing project: the rediscovery of lost energy to be found by going to the "green hills of Africa", then wavy, more northern inlets, bays topped by late-medieval castles, expanses of red heather and equally red land to delicately trample on and all far, far away from my native land (to be temporarily forgotten). All this has become a mirage, a distant morgana, a torn fabric which needs to be repaired, sewn, thread after thread, a weft and a warp to be reassembled manually, gently, slowly re-emerging from the tingling sensation that painfully echoes the paralysis of these long days.

Day sixty-one

Cautiously, in the afternoon we go out to the park, a long walk of about 7 kilometres, passing acres and acres of woods along the Pavia channel of

Vernavola, which unfolds from the outskirts of the city, like a placid snake with scales that glisten in the sun, to San Genesio ed Uniti and beyond. It's a wonderful walk across vast and almost deserted meadows, few passers-by, and, above all, the company of two of our dearest friends, whom we had not seen since the beginning of March. We converse amiably as we walk with our masks are always properly on our faces, keeping safety distances, with conversations that dive into and re-emerge from our past. Memories, thoughts, serene chatter, reflections on our children, while Ale does his break-dance jumping front flip on the green meadows, leaving us breathless. Walking is fantastic. Sweating is nice. One of my friends is my tennis partner, and we talk about the possibility of resuming my favourite sport. He's still suffering from a slight sprain of his right wrist, which slightly dampens my mood, but we won't be able to start right away because the courts are still closed. Then, I think to myself, we have wide open fields in front of us, and a future to fill with life. That's the important thing. We see incredible fields of red poppies that seem to be red streaked waves rippled by the wind. The sky is a little bit cloudy. A poem by Whitman comes to mind, I can't remember its name, but it talks about a walk during which even a blade of grass seems to represent the entire universe. I think about how difficult it is to convey this love for the mystery of everything surrounding us.

Day sixty-two

Today, perhaps because it's Sunday (10 May 2020), it is a day to reflect on the "return to normality". Although gradually, of course. In addition to my private practice with patients, I should resume supervising at the Swiss Neuropsychiatric Services in Canton Ticino. I speak to friends and colleagues who tell me that tomorrow they will resume travelling for work, also in other provinces or even regions. However, at the moment, when I think of resuming, I perceive my mind as if it were a rusty tool that needs to be oiled before I can make it work. A bit as if my mind was infiltrated by the doubt of no longer being able to work as I did before the lockdown. This was strange because my work had always come naturally for me. What helped was when I remembered that I had sprained my left calf, years ago, during a tennis match. I was confined in a plaster cast from the knee down for about a month in the so-called "equine posture". It was a hell of an experience. I had to do intensive physiotherapy to simply put my foot on the ground. Only after about three months of physical therapy did I get better, but I still found it difficult to put my foot on the ground and walk normally. Afterwards I also resumed playing tennis normally, which seemed impossible at the time of the accident on the court, beyond recovery. Mentally, I seem to relive the same sensations of that time, almost as if I needed to go through a psychic rehabilitation in making (mental) movements that seemed natural to me before the "accident". A bit like Oliver Sacks in his beautiful book *A Leg to Stand On*, when he talks about his experience as a doctor who became a patient due to a leg injury. Or like that time, at the age of 40, when Michele gave me chickenpox, which still now causes me to have shingles and different eye disorders. It happened in August. That experience was infernal as well: the August heat, together with herpetic pustules, fever and cervical pains, was a real physical massacre and it took me more than a month to recover. In short, I am describing, as you can easily understand, how fragile our bodies can be. And just remember, the body, as Winnicott says, is the fundamental ground on which the mind grows. I feel I need to seriously reflect on these considerations when I think of the "return to normality".

Day sixty-three

I continue my reflections on the "return to normality", on the reopening of studies. The problem is that even in these days I continue to hear at least six ambulances with sirens blaring each day. They are not few, and don't seem to be to related to road accidents see ... I discuss this with some colleagues on the phone. One of them, from Milan, "scolded" me firmly just by pointing out my pale desire to see the patients in person again. She is not alone, another colleague tells me that she will not reopen until late September: she will see all the patients on Skype and WhatsApp video calls. By the way, I am now doing the same for some group and individual supervisions. Today is Monday: I heard at least three ambulances in the morning. The day is not over yet. Today the rain is pouring and freezing winds are blowing, making it seem like November again. This climate is neither heartening nor reminiscent of "reopening". I think about the fact that these days seem like "alternating currents". Sometimes you feel like running towards a self-styled "normality", but then you go back and self-impose the initial restrictions of the lockdown, because you hear that around you, among your acquaintances, colleagues, distant relatives, there are at least 50 or 60 people who have had the disease, or are positive and asymptomatic. The young son of another colleague, who worked as a doctor in a rest home for a few months now, is at home with a fever. The colleague is very worried and I am also. "Luckily he is young and maybe he is immunized", she says, but her voice on the phone betrays an emotion that only parents with children can fully understand. We need to stay still in this era, after a pause, I think that we'll have time to run later. But just walking alone would be great. On the other hand, it is certain that a return to normality would truly be appreciated today, between bad connections, unstable wi-fi, conflicts between Zoom and Skype.

Day sixty-four

There's dust on my desk in the studio. I have to clean it up. It means time is passing, no sign of humans passing by, sitting in front of me, for about 30 years from now. Besides my fantasies of transience, all the patients don't seem remotely affected by the setting – I notice it more and more every day. In each session, beyond the obvious individual differences, it seems to me there is the same free associative trend of a session in person. I do not really see any substantial differences, that is, it is as if the body was represented equally "in effigy" by the voice, and even amplified by the images on the screen. On the contrary, the body is even more intrusive, since the screen of the PC enlarges the body. Of course, there is also the absence, but I don't think that this absence seems to take on the form of a persecutory object. On the contrary, some patients tell me, very clearly, that they feel continuity: this continuity is essential, for them (and for me). Seeing each other in person then seems to be more invasive and deforming to the setting than a Skype mode. Being in person with masks, eventual sheets to be spread on the couch, a wider space between the armchair and couch than before, successive "sanitizations" of the studio, etc., result, for many patients, as obstructing objects, which generate fantasies of a de-animation of the session, which would really become inhabited by inanimate objects, precisely because they are too "real". Analysis is concerned with internal reality. External reality must be put in brackets. What sense does it make to bring an FFP2 mask into the analysis room? Of course, it is now customary to bring mobile phones into the session, for example, something that in my analytic days was not even conceivable, but because they did not exist. In fact, teenagers bring various objects into the session, like the time when a 15-year-old girl had a session with me and put makeup, nail polish and mascara on my desk (did she want to show me her nails in the transference?). But these "concrete objects" are something else, they are subjective objects. Not a mask. Instead, it is an anonymous, impersonal object, which refers to a homologated, sanitary, extraneous reality, which does not belong to the subject. Being "remote" is subjective, or rather it is perhaps what allows us to oscillate between subjective and objective, between *alibi et tunc* and *hic et nunc*.

Day sixty-five

Some days, like today pass calmly and I seem to glimpse clearings of happiness that one could not imagine in a period like this. Today I didn't even hear an ambulance, and in spite of the grey, rainy and icy weather, this simple gift of silence comforted me quite a bit. I had many sessions and I thought that Bion was really right when he said that the patient is "the best colleague". I also think of colleagues as "best colleagues". I also see them in several meetings on Zoom, which I think continues to be a very good platform, because it lets you see people as if you were in a room, talking with even more fluidity than sometimes in a live meeting. These experiences today are then linked to the email received in these days from the Scientific Secretary of the SPI, Massimo Vigna Taglianti, who informs us that the National Italian Psychoanalytic Society Congress – where I should have brought a paper – which was to be held at the end of May, and then moved to October, is now postponed to February 2021. This increases my feeling of suspended uncertainty, although I also think that the so-called "scientific activity" has not been suspended at all within the individual local psychoanalytic microcosms. Yesterday evening I participated, for example, in a very interesting seminar of the Psychoanalytic Centre of Pavia, held by Anna Maria Fiamminghi, on the theme of the "fraternal dimension". The seminar made me see even more clearly that, beyond the institutions and their rites and rituals, psychoanalysts continue thinking vivaciously. But in addition to this, it made me reflect on the fact that perhaps this seminar was perfect for these days, given the topic proposed. The "fraternity", alas. Beyond "governments", noble fathers, paternalisms, third parties, may be the container that holds, works and transforms is precisely represented by fraternal relations, groups of brothers. Something similar probably also happens to Italians, I thought: despite the leaders who guide them or who would like to guide them, despite their competence or incompetence, perhaps Italians have always made it because they are a "group of brothers", perhaps quarrelsome, chaotic and variegated (as brothers all are, moreover) that keep the nation going, notwithstanding the ineptitude of those in command. Take, for instance the Lombard Healthcare System. In spite of Formigoni, Maroni, Fontana, Gallera our doctors and nurses were the pillars that "held" up the system and cared for the population of an entire region. They too, like my colleagues, feel like brothers. And for that, but not only that, I thank them.

Day sixty-six

I feel a fresh gust of happiness in talking about diseases other than those related to Covid-19, with the four doctor patients of today. One of them talks to me the whole session about tuberculosis: it was diagnosed in his ward in a young woman. "I couldn't believe I was dealing with a case of tuberculosis, a normal, known, treatable case!" he tells me almost in tears. I discover that I am also happy to talk about sanatoriums, bacteria, anti-tubercular vaccines, bronchoscopies, instead of coronavirus. Finally, you can enter new rooms, in cleaner "wards" more "clean", less intoxicated by stray beta elements like bullets, like bombs of anguish that too often I have perceived whizzing by too closely in these last two months. We can speak of tuberculosis! Hurray! The number of hospitalizations is decreasing, it seems we can return to a more normal daily healthcare, where you can deal with cystitis with a sense of tender familiarity. Perhaps the Uncanny is moving away, everyone tells me. Another doctor tells me about an elderly patient of his, Esterina, who at 94 years of age, positive for the virus, then recovered. "Just think how strange life is." Another one needs to evoke the anguish he lived in the days when he had to visit positive patients. Then, all the stories, curiously enough, converge on lashing out fierce criticism towards the Lombardy Region, its insufficiencies, the chaos in decision-making, guidelines that keep changing. A colleague who works in a counselling centre for adolescents in Lombardy tells me that the director of her Asst (Local health service facility) has moved her counselling centre into a dark basement, where there is no connection. She is forced to go out and have interviews and psychotherapy with WhatsApp video calls in her car. She tells me that the medium- to long-term project is to dismantle public counselling centres to facilitate the development of private services, especially Catholic-run ones. The director of his Asst (Local health service facility) happens to be a director of Comunione e Liberazione.[4] Yes, it's much more interesting to talk about tuberculosis.

Day sixty-seven

I put on about two kilograms during this lockdown. This is also the sign of something strange since I am constitutionally very thin. I only happen to gain weight on vacation, or on rare occasions of relaxation or very prolonged sedentariness – for example when I was writing my dissertation, but I was 25 years old at the time – but at most one kilogram or little more. I had never gained two extra kilos in two months. My wife is happy about it, she has never seen me so well fed. Not that you can see it at a glance, actually, because I still have a thin, wiry physique despite my weight gain. But it is this unusual trend in my metabolism that puzzles me. I usually have a very good appetite, but I probably consume the calories I ingest almost immediately because I normally move much more than now, although part of my day is spent behind a couch, sitting in an armchair. Moreover, Alessandro has introduced a whole series of new vegetarian dishes in the family in the last few months, so I am not whatsoever bombarded with carbohydrates. Nor do I drink a lot of alcohol, although I enjoy a wee bit of beer every now and then. But it has to be good and even better if it is homemade, otherwise I always prefer natural water by far. It seems, that is, that the allostatic lockdown has had physical side-effects on me too, to the point that I have had to equip myself with an anti-decubitus pillow that I use when I sit behind the couch. This decision came naturally to me, given my bony constitutional. In fact, I don't usually like to sit on straight wooden chairs, because I risk having a sore bum, and I try to do as much physical activity: standing, walking anything to move my poor muscles (mind you the best would be tennis) as this locked-up situation permits. I don't dare imagine, what would happen to my weight form if I stopped smoking, in this cloistered situation. I'm going to light a cigarette right now.

Day sixty-eight

"Unthought Known", that's the concept that comes to mind all day long. A term that the English psychoanalyst Christopher Bollas coined in 1987 in his book *The Shadow of the Object*, reprinted in a new edition expanded by Raffaello Cortina in 2018. I thought of it in relation to the new sensations and new fears that we are experiencing in these months. That is, I wondered if they are really new fears, or if they may be the reverberation of an "unthought known" of the individual and the group, of the society. After all, for all of us, suddenly, the Italian State as a public institution has become a sort of idealized protective mother who has furnished us with guidelines, proxemics limits, i.e. a "holding" and "handling" within a circumstance that could become much more dangerous for everyone. We are not only what we are now, but we are also what we have been, and some traumatic circumstances can make us regress to states of mind that not only make us "feel" like frightened children, but that may actually make us "become" such. In two words this is the essence of the "unthought known". In more generative and serene situations, the individual enters into himself, experiencing a contact with his child Self, increasing the possibility of knowing what has constituted his intrinsic known unthought. The experience of the contagion and the epidemic has brought us into contact, regressively, with this child Self, both individually and as a society. We can explain the specific nature of the fears that we have lived and are living from this type of intra- and inter-psychic context: a regression to very primitive paranoid anxieties, which made us relive the "unthought known" of an absolute anguish of separation and collapse. This anguish can be translated into the sudden, humanly shared awareness that we are all orphans, that is, that we no longer have our idealized maternal protection. Social "distancing", confinement, quarantine, have only intensified these primitive anxieties as "evocative objects" (Bollas, 2010). How can the child within us feel the contact and warmth of the maternal breast if he is wearing a mask?

Day sixty-nine

Today, after more than two months, I go out for a "take away aperitif" with Luigi. It is an alienating experience: we go to a brewery that we usually frequent in the evening, after dinner, in Pavia, in Via dei Mille, not far from Ponte Vecchio, over the Ticino River which has been flowing for centuries, unaware of any human incident in history, let alone a bothersome (yet lethal) virus. The brewery is closed, so we head towards Ticino. We finally find another one. From 4 May until today, only a few sparse local bars are open but close on the dot at 7.30 p.m. and only for takeaway beers. The sun is hot, some young guys are hanging out on the sidewalks of the tree-lined avenue. I begin to feel a sense of ambivalence. On the one hand, I am happy to see Luigi again, on the other hand I feel like a chill running up my spine as I cross the street heading to a place that was previously very familiar to me. I don't know why seeing all these people with masks, like me, disturbs me, yet also simultaneously transmits a transcendent sense of vitality. I have some trouble keeping together these apparently contradictory thoughts like trying to mix water with oil. They don't amalgamate, there is no mixture, the two elements move away from each other. It seems like the chemistry of things is not reassuring but centrifugal and elusive. Then I also meet Stefano, a friend and colleague. I have the same feeling again: I am very happy to meet friends I haven't seen for a long time, but seeing him with the surgical mask makes me feel strange. Extraneity? Alterity? I promise myself I will find the time and the mental space to think about it. I believe that friends have an important psychic function, that is it helps each of our egos in confirming the sense of our own temporal and affective continuity. They confirm one's own sense of cohesion, given precisely by continuity. Today it is different, there is continuity but also discontinuity in these encounters, and maybe it is this strange mélange between permanence and breaking of a continuum that makes me perceive this afternoon outing as perturbing. Luigi and I, after a short stop at the brewery, cross the old bridge on foot. I am moved by Borgo Ticino and the red bricks of the bridge. It seems a century since I've seen them. In Piazza della Vittoria we also meet Francesco. We have known each other for 30 years and the three of us sit on the steps of the Broletto and chat. We are always the same, I know that, and it is good to see each other. But we are also different. This virus has changed us.

Day seventy

My wife is sick and tired of remote teaching. Spending hours correcting homework from fifth graders who send photographs of crumpled, unreadable sheets of paper via WhatsApp or Zoom or Meet tends to be a mystic experience in the long run. A kind of neo-Sufism during in which you feel like you are part of Mevlana's Dervishes. In this regard, I recommend my teacher friends to watch Ari Aster's film *Midsommar* (2019), set in a Swedish community where tribal rituals are consumed at the limit of a mystical–hallucinatory experience. The final sequence of the ritual dance of the girls covered in flowers, who then fall to the ground exhausted, is a masterpiece. Anna, a dear teacher friend of mine, after three months of remote teaching, writes this on her Facebook page:

> I turned off the computer at 1.36 am at night after 3 hours of lessons and 6 hours of corrections on my PC, in possession of my physical and mental faculties, not so much, I solemnly SWEAR: for the school year 2020–2021, with or without remote teaching, I will NEVER correct blurred photographs of homework done on sheets of kitchen paper, that are torn, greasy, and drooled on by dogs; nor photographs of homework photographed with a bird's eye view subject to monstrous optical distortions; nor photographs of texts written on computer, photographed and sent in separate pages; nor tampered, unnamed image files; and photographs of sparse unnumbered, disordered pages, I really broke my balls.

The text seems to be an admirable example, which illustrates teachers' state of mind clearly. These teachers have been left alone to manage large social groups and moreover in full pre-adolescence and adolescence stages of life, within an epochal and fatiguing quarantine. Moreover, yesterday I also had a face-to-face session with a patient teenager, immersed in a noisy background of dogs barking furiously, screaming mothers and car horns blasting under the girl's house. Thank goodness summer vacation isn't far away. Is it the "hate in countertransference", dear Winnicott?

Day seventy-one

Today was convulsive. I thought these days were by now part of the first and now distant stage of the epidemic. But they don't seem to be. In the meantime, my wife has to go back to the hospital again, she has to queue up in crowded clinics just for a simple blood test. Then I get a call from a colleague at the SPDC who wants to send me cases of pre-psychotic teenagers with symptoms exacerbated by this lockdown. She says that, at the moment, the ward is full of agitated patients, many of whom are adolescents with social withdrawal syndromes. Prior to hospitalization these kids spent all day at home, without contacts, immersed in video games, apps, social, and at some point developed delusional symptoms. The quarantine certainly didn't help. In the afternoon a young intern from the same SPDC called me again for another case similar to those mentioned above. I feel like I've been enlisted by the Territorial Psychiatric Services. In the past, I've received requests from the CPS (Local Psychiatry Out-patient Clinic), but they were sporadic. Now the pressure is increasing, like a long wave of the Spirit of Time (Zeitgeist) that is coming at me relentlessly. I am reminded of the famous phrase pronounced by Roy Batty (Rutger Hauer) in *Blade Runner*: "I have seen things you humans couldn't imagine, battleships on fire off the ramparts of Orion, and I have seen B-rays flash in the dark near the gates of Tannhäuser." Some days are wavering, then there are other days in which the waters are troubled, like this one. You must hold the rudder firmly in your hand and keeping a careful distance from the rocks. Images come to mind as reveries and you must follow them as they unfold, give them the dreamy weight they require, make them concave and wait for them to make sense, when needed, when they become clearer. And then you must put together these images of films, of stories, of myths, to try to create an alphabet that becomes grammar and language that serves to describe, to narrate, to give voice to the future.

Day seventy-two

I believe that during this tragic pandemic event, humanity is experiencing the unconscious, in a way – perhaps – that could be similar to that of the experience that occurs in analysis. One of the prerequisites of the long process of becoming an analyst, not by chance, in fact, consists in having experienced the unconscious during one's own analysis. To "experience the unconscious" means to know how to stop in a foundational absence, in a void of certainties, in a state of feeling confused and crossed by an otherness that we do perceive as being ours but that is ours. Experiencing a foundational absence means above all confronting oneself with an unknown, an "impossible", which perhaps we could also define by the term "unheard of". Are we not living an unprecedented experience? Never "heard" before (with all our senses, not only with hearing)? That has broken down the sense of our habitual inclination to represent the things we were living? Actually "things" are and have always been where they are, eternally unattainable. But it is our stable representation of them that makes us perceive the sense of existing. Here, instead, something previously stabilizing has broken: everything has been suspended and modified in a "sine die" that will not allow us, however, to rewind the film and go back to the starting point. We climbed up a long, very long ladder and when we arrived at the top, we threw the ladder away. It's impossible to descend to where we climbed up from. It is this "impossible", the unheard of, the unknown that the epidemic forced us to meet. There is no "phase 2" or "phase 3", because in reality we are now in an Area X, the unknown of an equation that we do not know how to solve because the future mathematician capable of solving it has not been born yet. We are constricted to stop here in this new land that has never seen before, that is in fact new, auroral, worrying and Uncanny. This absence must pass through us. Perhaps it is time to think about a new ontology, a new sense of Being. And this seems terrible, frightening to us. To experience the unconscious, in the end, is to experience the not-like-before.

Day seventy-three

I have decided to conclude this diary on the day when I will start seeing the first patient in the studio again, in person. I think I will go in stages: first I will see the teenagers, who have all remained hermetically sealed in their homes, just like me, some like canned sardines and autistic–contiguous to their parents that have been exhausted by an unprecedented proximity, young wildflowers needy of oxygen to grow, constricted in a sultry greenhouse. One of them has developed a terrible stiff neck that she has never had and is preparing to graduate in the living room of her house with the graduation committee via Zoom. Another one learned how to sew and make shirts "with daddy's old shirts". A young man in his first years of university can't wait to return to the university library: "at least there I am alone, in my own space, and everyone there is silent and I won't feel my parents' and my sister's breathing down my neck …". I too am with him in my study and we are surrounded by the reassuring silence of the books on my bookshelves. I think that giving back the physical and concrete space of my studio to these teenagers is as urgent as giving them back the possibility to experience a specific space of mental growth, not mediated or crammed into the tunnels of dangling earphones, of telephone lines that pass through the anonymous jointures of the telephone fiber distribution hubs. A true, live, tangible and habitable space, for the spirit, not only for the body. I will see the doctors last: I have already talked to some of them and they all agree. I still can't imagine what the first meeting with the patients will be like after this sort of Chandlerian "long goodbye".

Day seventy-four

Patients are starting to talk about seeing each other live, when we will see each other, how we will see each other. Curiously today these conversations seem to be mediated by free associations concerning cartoons and comics. One young patient in particular fills the emotional field with stories about Diabolik, the man masquerading together with his blonde girlfriend. When we see each other, and have masks, will we all look like Diabolik? Will we be able to use the couch right away? Or just the armchairs? So many questions, so many doubts, springing up inside me like internal thermal waters, that I still don't know how and where to channel. I think I'll let myself be guided, once again, by reverie, by my preconscious, you can call it whatever you prefer. I confess to myself that I am sailing on sight on this subject. I set 8 June as the date for the start of commencement of work of a gradual resumption in the studio, but I don't really, profoundly know what it means to me. I imagine I twill take a long time to elaborate all this with the patients in the studio and in person. That is, to understand what happened, what it actually was, to restart the engines of thinking a thought about this time that was fractured, about this dyschromic wall that has suddenly imposed itself on us. Other cartoons, for example Walt Disney's *Pinocchio*, compared to that by Garrone, then *Finding Nemo*, the clownfish that lost its mother who his father looks for in the swirling waters of the Australian sea currents, together with his friend Dory, a fish with a short-term memory loss. Nemo in the aquarium, locked inside the dentist's office, waiting to be freed with the help of his friends, and the starfish. All free associations that refer to becoming "a real child", from a wooden puppet always struggling with a darkness, with an abyss that seems to want to swallow him at every step: Fire Eater, the Whale, the Cat and the Fox. A coerced True self only longing for a place to exist.

Day seventy-five

Today being Saturday, Ale and I resume our film project as we wait for a "shot" that is still unknown to us; we haven't yet imagined it, so we are waiting for reality to take shape. It's time for the audio. We both agree on the jazz genre, Woody Herman in particular. Before we get down to business, I'm attending an IIPG[5] seminar on *The Uncanny*, invited by a colleague from Bologna. We talk about my book: it is comforting and rewarding to hear colleagues from Ancona, Rome and other parts of Italy who have read my book and quote it during a seminar with more than a hundred participants. In the afternoon Ale and I return to our favourite hobby. We like the short film, it is going well. We are doing the editing, the fades are at the right point. We chat all afternoon always about "fades". What "fades", I wonder, what "fades" are we talking about? Or do we want to take another form from the elimination of another? Woody Herman's notes are rippling through the air, sending us back to following an élan vital, inviting us to dive into it, like Nemo's turtles in the Gulf Stream. A very strong current, which stuns and turns the little sea turtles upside down, but then invigorates them, makes them feel stronger. Perhaps, I feel it is the time of that freshness that is "fading" as a transient precognition. *Panta rei* and Ale want to stop this time in the frames, this lingering, which then, perhaps, is always a fading that lingers.

Day seventy-six

I am quite disturbed when I find out that I have an early stage "compression injury" in the sacral area. These micro lesions are part of the broader range of physical deformities that are part of the so-called "immobilization syndrome". This syndrome affects people who are bedridden or sitting for a long time, or who do not do any type of physical movement. The areas most affected are mainly the sacral area, but also trochanteric regions, heels, scapular regions, ankles. And particularly thin and bony people, like myself, are affected. In fact, I had to buy myself an anti-decubitus cushion to use for my analyst armchair of the couch, that I sit on many hours a day, And the quarantine has accentuated a problem that was not present at all months ago. In fact, I was thinking that I have been doing this absolutely sedentary job for at least 30 years and this problem is the result. But I really didn't expect a "compression injury" at the age of 55. Luckily, my tennis partner seems to have overcome his wrist problem, so we will finally be able to resume tennis at least as soon as they open the courts and/ or you can play outdoors. Leaving these slightly melancholic thoughts behind, today is Sunday, and is cheerfully passed by visiting with dear friends of ours who come to see us and we all eat a pizza together on the terrace. It doesn't seem real to us that we can see each other again and we seem to have so many things to say that we all talk at the same time, almost overwhelming ourselves with words. We look at each other and say "I see that you have put on some kilos", or "you have to go on holiday as soon as possible, you seem a little tired", and so on, as if we were in an unconscious process of mutual psychic recognition leading us to also recognize the continuity of ourselves.

Day seventy-seven

I begin to mentally adjust myself to the great manoeuvres of "psychoanalytic phase 2". Considering the national and Lombard epidemic trend, considering my gradual outings into the world, the small doses of finally seeing friends and relatives, and considering that daily flow of things around me seems to be more serene (supermarkets full of people, but moving with the prescribed precautions, cars circulating, no ambulance sirens for several days now), I did it. I decided to see only one first patient on Thursday, 4 June, and then proceed with almost all the others from Monday, 8 June. Of course now, the practical aspects are at the top of the agenda: how to sanitize the study? How to reorganize the agenda so that between one patient and another, at least an abundant 15 minutes can pass to ventilate and disinfect the spaces? This dimension is also completely new, never encountered before, and it moves emotions to which I cannot give a name. How will the patient see me? What will it be like to see ourselves "in person"? But then, above all, what will be the new meanings of the term "in person"? I don't think it will have anything to do with the "concrete" aspect of being there, in flesh and blood. I mean it won't only be that. "In person" will mean a lot of things that have yet to be discovered.

Day seventy-eight

"The kids are starting to hug each other", says a patient lying on my virtual couch. Her six-year-old son met a friend of his at the playground and, after almost three months of not seeing each other, he says, "I missed you. Come on, shall we hug?" Luckily the two mothers present are not particularly anxious, and the two children can finally start playing together again. There is the sensation of lost objects that are now found. Yes, it's in the air these days, a sea breeze is starting to rise and touch us with slight but evident signs of leavening new beginnings. The theme of "leavening" comes up unexpectedly also in another session, during which a patient with two adult offspring, at home with her since the start of the lockdown, talks to me at length about the homemade bread that they made together: manitoba flour, durum wheat flour, and then, ah, yeast is fundamental. And the containers, the right baking pans to put the dough in, are of essential importance. The cast iron ones are exceptional and mind you, if you don't use the right container, the bread doesn't rise properly, and the dry yeast is fine, but be careful about the quality. Also the transfert, I think, needs time and the right ingredients to rise, as long as you find the right "cast iron baking pan", "to put the dough in". I am reminded of a distinguished colleague who often uses gastronomic metaphors, including cooking metaphors, and again, then a conference many years ago during which there was a memorable exchange between this colleague and another one, who was famous for his Freudian orthodoxy, who said: "You always talk about cooking, you seem like a chef with a chef's hat on your head." Today it seems to me that we are wearing a chef's hat: we cook gradual findings, movements and emotions that have been left too long, endlessly in a brine, closed in jars abandoned on dusty shelves. Now we can open the lids and smell the scent of children's hugs. For example, when I start telling my patients that we will see each other again in a week or two and they start talking to me about returning to restaurants, of bakeries near my office that they went to before or after the sessions, of gyms that re-open, of bread rising in hot ovens after delicately kneading the right mixture of flours.

Day seventy-nine

My heart took a plunge as soon as I call and hear the voice of the secretary of the Sports Center of the tennis courts where I have been training for years. I can play again! For months, a metal answering machine answered every time I called and said that the courts were closed until further notice. Now, instead, next Sunday I will feel the slippery red earth under my feet and my rubber shoes slipping sideways while I swing a forehand or a backhand. Every time I set foot on a tennis court it's as if the tape of an old VHS inside me rewinds and makes me go back to when I was 12 years old and played with my middle-school mates for the first time with those heavy wooden rackets on the streets of the working-class neighbourhood on the outskirts of Pavia where I lived. In the Quartiere Scala, just behind the football field, there were huge asphalted and empty spaces, right next to the new public housing complexes just built in the sixties. Right there, we are undisturbed by unwanted onlookers in our magical tennis "utopia", drawing lines on the ground with red bricks. Even without a net we felt like we were at Wimbledon, surrounded by canals where frogs croaked and fireflies danced silently in the evening. We watched them, as if hypnotized, turning on and off in the dark. I know that on Sunday I will remember and relish those memories, especially after these withered dull, and rachitic months. Psychological births and rebirths.

Day eighty

Around the world in 80 days. I feel like Phileas Fogg, except for not bearing his high lineage and not in possession of the trusted Jean Passepartout, in this journey made of words and emotions that began on 10th March. I feel that the journey is coming to an end, that the trolley is coming out of the cockpit, that the balloon is coming down and that the pilot is looking where to land. A French landing? A more classic landing? I can see clear skies for now, the visibility is good. There are no high-voltage pillars on the horizon. When landing, a sudden gust of wind near pillars can be very dangerous, and the pilot knows it. I can't see any of these metal beams at the moment, the wind is soft and the ground seems flat. Even the patients' dreams begin to whisper thoughts that gaze in the direction of seeing each other again in the studio. A young girl dreams that she is hiding in a shopping mall, while an elephant chases her: "but I'm also strangely too fat, and even though I'm hiding behind a pillar, I know the elephant can see me ...". This thought of a "return to normality" can be cumbersome. This body–mind that for months hid behind columns of pixels and crackling decibels along the wires of earphones or in the speakers of the PC now shows itself again in its naked authenticity. As the patient speaks to me, I am reminded of the Latin term "*larvatus prodeo*" (I show myself by with a mask) which is Paul Ricoeur's definition of dreams (P. Ricoeur, "On Interpretation". Essay on Freud, 1965). In a similar way, Bion speaks about the emergence of the unconscious through the concealment of what the dream figured in sleep or waking. "Larvatus prodest" – I tell myself that transference cannot also hide behind a toothpick, behind a banal shopping mall pillar. And not even in the virtual distance of a Skype video call. At the end of the day, I think that if Jules Verne were here today, he would have had a lot of material to work on to write about other trips, other "world tours", other twenty thousand leagues under the seas.

Day eighty-one

I am increasingly convinced that the doctors who have faced the months of collapse of Lombardy's healthcare system, once having overcome the initial "manic phase" which was activated inside themselves to survive those terrible days, will soon be suffering a post-traumatic return of that emotional bombardment. One of my doctor patients throughout the session, almost in tears, tells me about some of his colleagues who have had panic attacks in recent days. Right now, he tells me, that the workload has decreased considerably, the intensive therapies are emptying out and work is back to normal (even though the 12-hour shifts in the ward are still the same). Nobody in his hospital is interested in the emotional implications of what the staff has been going through during these months. Then he says to me: "I feel lucky, and I thank you. It's a good thing that I've always been able to continue analysis on Skype, otherwise I don't know how I would have made it." This phrase touches me and deeply moves me. This patient will not come to the studio until at least September. He doesn't feel up to it: "It's strange, I feel more protected in the hospital. When I go out and just go to the supermarket I get tachycardia and sometimes I have to go home and my wife has to go for me." I think he and I will have to work on this new problem. And we will work on it, on Skype, for several more months. This patient, in pre-Covid times, has always been a sportsman, a vital person, but it seems that this trauma has reactivated old areas in him, moved and disarticulated "emotional floors" that I thought had been stabilized in analysis. Many doctors also seem to have altered their perception of time. Another patient remembers the days of Covid-19 and tells me: "In those days I no longer had any sense of time. I was doing sixty hours a week, people were dying in front of me. I understood more or less what time it was only by the rising and setting of the sun. Now if I ask my colleagues how many months have passed, they hesitate, don't remember, as if years had passed." Meanwhile, during the lockdown, new patients have asked me to start treatment. I agreed, although, at first, I was reluctant to do a first session remotely, I've never done it before, except for a patient living in Holland. Then I will start seeing these patients in person again after 4th June. These new developments induce me to reflect on the emotional powerfulness ("Acheronta movebo" Freud wrote) of the epidemic. The huge viral load, is not only biological, but also psychic. Will we find the vaccine for both?

Day eighty-two

Today, I really feel like being outdoors, especially since today is Saturday. I realize that these last few months have been pretty tough as I leaf back through the pages of this diary, especially when I consider my wife's surgery, her complex convalescence, going to healthcare facilities in the middle of an epidemic, the radical change of setting with patients doing everything remotely, as well as the impact of worrying about some of my colleagues who have been seriously ill with Coronavirus. In the meantime, however, a new baby, a great-nephew is being born, the son of one of my many young nieces and nephews living around the world. He's coming to light these very days, and I'm delighted.

I'm going out with Ale and I can feel a pleasant light wind snipping at my face. Let's go and buy a roll of paper to cover the couch, since next week I will begin seeing the first patients in the studio, with all the necessary precautions, of course. I have long conversations on the phone with dear colleagues and we share fears, doubts, perplexities, but also hopes and above all desire to meet and go out to lunch or dinner together. Restlessness and the need for new beginnings, together with a sense of bewilderment seem to be asking to be shared and elaborated. Another colleague writes to me that she is getting married tomorrow, but that she will of course postpone the celebrations to a more suitable date. "Lots of stuff", as my teenage patients would say, but "it fits", as they would then comment in their fluid slang spoken and written on Instagram, or of the many other social networks. I am very grateful to them, having accompanied me in this complex and laborious journey just as I have tried to the best of my ability to accompany them on their road towards growth, on this stretch of the road of life that has suddenly become very rough, for all of us.

Day eighty-three

Tennis. Sunday: on the same day that Edoardo, my new great-nephew, was born, I start playing tennis again. It seems like a very special, magical situation. Actually, it reminds me of the German TV series *Dark*, all focused on time slippage. Ale has started watching it recently and I join him sometimes. I am amazed by how fluid my movements are while I play tennis, probably well anchored in my implicit memory. After five minutes of feeling rusty, on the

62 Angelo Antonio Moroni

court flooded by a beautiful sun at the end of May, I begin to move as in a dance and rediscover the rhythm as I twirl around with my foot firmly on the ground. The line of the net suddenly becomes a rediscovered reference point, a meta-psychic guarantor, a symbolic, anthropological, essential and powerful form of Being. It seems like a century that I haven't set foot on a court and even my tennis partner is particularly surprised that we can play easily and move freely, almost as if a year and not three months have passed since the last time we played. It's nice to firmly grip the racket and lift the ball and see it fly lightly over the net. They forecast sun in the next few days. I want to take advantage of this great weather. So I make plans, I would love to go horseback riding in the hills. Maybe I'm exaggerating, but then again I really can't wait to see the delicate hairpin bends of the Oltrepò Pavese hills again.

Day eighty-four

I had a nice lunch with Michele, my almost 20-year-old son, at the Road House. I expected to find a deserted place with a sparse few trembling frightened people, an obvious projection of my own doubts and fears hatched during these three months of forced cloister. Instead, I find small groups of young people and families (never more than three per table) chatting pleasantly. The two of us also savour a sense of peaceful rest and pleasure. We talk about future projects about our differences, as father and son in our professional ideals. Michele thinks about a future in "music marketing", something completely alien to me, more or less like studying medieval Armenian language would be. "Hey, but you can't think that if you've wanted to be a psychoanalyst since the age of 12, then OTHER PEOPLE have to follow in your footsteps." And he's right, I answer him. "The others", indeed. Children are "others" to you, and thank goodness. I think that Michele is teaching me a lot of things today, in this shady place, while nice waitresses ask us if we are going to eat tartare or a bowl of basmati rice. He's teaching me to respect his otherness, which is also looking towards the future, towards a subjective evolution, the generative dawn of a beginning Self. His, differentiated and yet multiform hypseity is beginning to walk. He must do the musical "marketing" of himself, begin to write the score of his inner music, listen to it and translate it into the right melody. We move towards lighter and more common ground, we talk about rappers, about Post Malone, about Dani Faiv, who he sometimes makes me listen to when we are in the car together, with the Bluetooth phone connection. "You should listen to the new freestyle-Covid", Michele says as we arrive at the café.

Day eighty-five

The Oltrepò hills have a regenerating effect on me. They represent an inner landscape, a dwelling place for my spirit: I have been visiting them since my parents had a house in the hills, Near the village of Zavattarello, where I used to spend entire summers, during the period of primary school. Vast woods of majestic chestnut trees overlooked our house, and there was a well with a bucket and pulley, which had a mysterious sort of charm and curiosity for me. What could be at the bottom of the well? Those moments, with the image of the well led me to later draw a personal analogy between the well and the preconscious. The "preconscious", an enigmatic and equally fascinating concept of psychoanalysis, internal elsewhere, but close to consciousness, from which the so-called "derivatives of the unconscious" move, albeit always in their veiled seclusion, towards consciousness (this is what they told us during the training at the Centro Milanese di Psicoanalisi "Cesare Musatti"). Today I prefer to think of it as a dreamlike function of the mind, a psychic "tail of the eye", or as a sensitive ear perceiving the sounds of water gurgling up from the well. The echo of these old sounds I heard today on the hills around Zavattarello, walking in the sunny alleys of hidden precious, little villages, with names never heard of before: Perducco, Sette Borghi, Montelungo. As precious as the time spent with our exquisite dear friends who have always invited us up those streets. It's been too long since I have been able to stop and lay down under a tree, lost while looking at how the wind slowly transforms the shapes of the clouds, surrendering myself to the discreet appearance of the Being discretely appearing. I also feel like I can change (my) shape like a cloud in the blowing wind.

Day eighty-six

I find myself having truly new and mixed emotions as I organize my office to be able to meet my first patient tomorrow, finally in person. Meanwhile, The government term "Social Distancing" comes to mind. Why do they use the adjective "social"? The distance needed to avoid possible and hopefully avoidable probabilities of contagion is physical, not social. In my opinion confusing physical and social distancing is quite serious, as well as emblematic of the times we live in. On the contrary, we are in an era in which, like the air that we breathe we are in dire need of "social rapprochement", that is, special attention towards relations, solidarity, an attention, towards our "neighbour". "Love your neighbour as yourself", says one of the Ten Commandments, and loving your neighbour is the opposite of keeping him distant. I try to reflect on what will happen tomorrow when I and my patient will meet, both of us closed in our homes for three months. Fortunately she has a garden. I have already sent her some technical notes on what preventive procedures we should follow, according to the guidelines of the Region, and she responded enthusiastically, as if I invited her to dive into a new totally unedited emotional experience. Her reaction makes me understand that I have created a good alliance with this patient, because she trusts me and she feels I will firmly hold her hand tomorrow as we dive together. In the meantime, I'm starting to think of images of an airplane landing. As I wrote a few days ago, the landing gear has long since come out of the cockpit and the "technical notes" that I send to the patients seem to be like the dialogue with the control tower. I signal the runway where we will descend, when we should fasten our seat belts, as we return after this trip where we have been suspended in the air. It's like when there is too much air traffic and the pilot announces a delay in the descent from the loudspeaker: "We are flying over the airport waiting to land." We are landing to get closer, not to get farther, I think to myself, but to get closer in a new, unprecedented way, that we have never tried before. However, we were close to each other even while we were navigating in. And I think this long flight went well for both of us, my patient and me.

Day eighty-seven

I feel like at the beginning of a movie, after the lights have gone out in the theatre when I hear the intercom ringing in the studio and the familiar noise of the elevator coming up to the third floor, then the slow and delicate footsteps of this young woman who I hear approaching the studio door from the corridor. We greet each other at the door, both wearing FFP2 mask and decide to shake hands (then we will use the sanitary gel I have on my desk). That's how the film begins, a mental cinema, a continuous inner staging, conscious and unconscious, made of images that appear to me today as if they were old and yellowed. "It seems strange to me to see the window and the wall of your studio actually here front of me, after having seen them on Skype all this time", the patient tells me. I don't speak: it's the silence that speaks between us. I also feel like I have a new perception of space. The couch seems far away, bigger, as in some of Magritte's paintings, with those tiny rooms where the objects are huge: apples, combs, huge glasses, all tall reaching the ceiling. I am reminded of *Alice in Wonderland*, when Alice drinks the potion that makes her so tall. Who's Alice here? The room is filled with dreams of mountain hikes where the patient gets lost in unknown woods, together with her boyfriend who she can't find in the bushes and brush that prevent her from walking. Maybe we are trying to find each other, I think, and we proceed in uncertain steps, trying to feel if the floor still holds. Memories of diving from high cliffs, of friends sitting on the banisters of the Ponte Vecchio that risk falling in the Ticino River. A great movement of birth trauma "affections–sensations", of grasping reflex tests, of Apgar indexes, of parachute reflexes, and reborn needs of tuning. Starting over again after an earthquake in the nursery can be difficult but it is always beautiful.

Day Eighty-eight

Supervision with the team of a Community for Juvenile Offenders via Zoom. It's been hard for kids and operators to stay hermetically close in the facility for these months. They all have tired faces, some are connected from home, they are in quarantine because they are positive, some from the Community, with their mask on that they take off just to talk. One of the professional educators tells me that he doesn't know how ten boys from the juvenile prison or other communities have managed to resist for almost three months without anything dangerous happening. In the past there have been assaults, fights, everything and more. He's used to these incidents. Nothing happened in these months of lockdown, a feeling of airy pneumatic emptiness reigned, a lot of insomnia, rap music during the night, tiring for some people during night shifts. I have been going there on a usual basis for many years now and everyone would love to see me in person, but organizational and distance issues still prevent this contact for at least two more weeks. In the meantime, yesterday I managed to see my first patient and I still have to metabolize the sense of the session, understand the deep effect it had on me. Other colleagues have also started to see patients these days and we exchange impressions on the phone or via Skype. We all agree that notwithstanding the discontinuity, we all perceived that there was a continuity in the relationship that the emotional contact was not lost at all, that the analysis went on. The last patient of the day, a doctor finally on vacation, is furious about the groups of "deniers" and "conspiracy theorists" that are emerging in these days in our country and are demonstrating in the squares. He tells me: "It is a real madness to deny that all these people have died in Lombardy in the last three months. It's an insult to all of us who have worked sixty hours a week. And we haven't worked all these hours because of a simple cold. I am very angry." "Yes, you should be very angry", I say.

Day eighty-nine

It's Saturday, so we decide to treat ourselves by going out to dinner. We choose to go to the "Vita" (Life) restaurant after a vivid family debate about where to go to for our treat, after several weeks of hard work. It seems to be an interesting choice, which came from a sort of Ogden-style Third Analytic, a product of the mind of my family group, not of only one of us in particular. A call to life, to carry on notwithstanding everything, with our boats scratched and dented by recent bad weather, along the course of the karstic rivers that run in each of us. We walk through the streets of Pavia, finally full of people, of young people, of teenagers eager for "Life" speaking/jabbering loudly unendingly. They jabber continuously even with masks on, even when they are in line in front of the restaurant while awaiting body temperature measurement absolutely necessary to be able to enter and savour, like us, a renewed possibility to Desire. Ale and I talk, I don't know why, about *The Divine Comedy*, about Carmelo Bene's *Lectura Dantis*: "When the flame came here …", we are reminded, in a curious way, of the myth of Ulysses. Cheerful chatter emerges from the restaurant which is adorned with candles and their bright flames flicker in the wind. The days when cities appeared to me as ghostly deserted cathedrals, post-apocalyptic sites, ghost towns or empty papier-mâché scenery of an improbable abandoned Hollywood set suddenly seem far away.

Maybe Ulysses comes to mind because we also felt like the Homeric character cast beyond the Pillars of Hercules, far from an apparently unreachable Ithaca, in the tragic days of the health emergency. On their voyage at sea, Ulysses and his companions reached the limits of human reason, they experienced despair and the impossibility of divine help, of his omniscient knowledge, an overwhelming fragility: "as long as the sea was enclosed over us".[6] Tonight we return to "Life" to try to return to Life.

Day ninety

Time to close up. I'll see most of the patients in the office tomorrow, obviously in person. Tomorrow I will also write the last page of this diary. Right from the beginning, I had decided not to reread what I was writing and what I had written so far. I wanted this to be an experiment, a sort of Dadaist "automatic writing", a letting go to a "stream of consciousness". I wanted to attempt something like a Virginia Woolf style lighthouse trip, but daily, diaristic, not at all organized, preformed. I never wrote anything in this form, maybe only when I was 12 years old, an old diary that I still keep and that talks about my first days in the new and mysterious environment of middle school. A precious object, an old memory that is very dear to me and shows me that I have always enjoyed writing. And in fact, it is still a real pleasure for me. This diary is an unconscious homage – who knows – to the "free associations" inaugurated by Freud, by Jung, a homage to the Fathers perhaps, to my teachers, and then to many others again, in the following years. I think this testimonial of mine will remain, and in some way, I feel was necessary. I believe that I owed it to my patients in the first place. I couldn't bear thinking that so much of their and our pain had been suffered in vain, trickling silently into the rivulets of the anonymous routines of everyday life. And in the meantime, I'd like to begin to thank everyone who has followed me on this inner journey, as Walt Whitman wrote: "The journey of the soul, not life alone." All those who have had the patience to read my words, to give me strength, to communicate their anguish, their fears, hopes, dreams, images, signs of theirs and my "disease of becoming", as Thomas Ogden would call it. So I'll see you tomorrow.

Day Ninety-one   8th June 2020

I don't know what to say. I feel a little lost. If I look back, I think of this diary as a film, "*Nuovo Cinema Paradiso*", in which I am Totò as a child, who enchanted, looks at the images on the big screen, while Alfredo, the projectionist, sets the machines in motion, and projects the film on the wall of a house in the town square. This film of mine comes to an end and the audience leaves the theatre. Outside the cinema, "normal" life resumes. The patients enter the studio and we look at each other with strange expressions: "Can I shake your hand?" the first patient of the day asks me, as if he wanted to make sure that I am not dead, that I have not vanished into thin air like in the film *The War of the Worlds* by Steven Spielberg. More film sequences come to me. Another patient who is an educator tells me that she didn't notice any difference between Skype and seeing each other in the studio, that it's the relationship with me that counts. I'm glad she says that. Then as she speaks, new characters emerge from disabled children left alone too much and for too long, or distracted parents that don't see and can't appreciate, the passion, that she has put in her work during the hard days of remote teaching. Unconscious equivalences loom in the shadow of my studio, while outside it rains, it's an unusual downpour for the month of June. Long sessions where both I and my patients feel we have to regain possession of the physical and mental space of the studio, of an internal world that becomes external and vice versa. I need to rediscover the ability to grasp the Third Analytic that is forming gradually and progressively in the emotional field generated by our minds at work. Other patients come onto the scene who talk to me about girlfriends leaving for European cities, dense mists of separation, aromas of detachment and reunion. The last patient of the day enters the studio and with her eyes that light up, she says: "Beautiful!", an exclamation that pleasantly surprises me. The patient ends the session with an image that touches me very deeply. She has discovered in these days, with astonishment, that a blackbird has made a nest on the balcony of her house. "It is an architecture of unimaginable intertwined straws, then those beautiful blue eggs, that break open after a few days and out come these tiny little birds, that then grew so quickly in just a week. The blackbird and its partner, kept coming and going, flying back and forth to bring food to their little ones." In the evening, once again I close the door of the studio. I think of this last page of the diary. I think of all its many pages and I imagine them flying away like the blackbirds of my patient, unfurled in the air by the wind. Will someone pick them up?

Notes

1 Servizio Psichiatrico di Diagnosi e cura: Psychiatric Emergency.
2 "Well imagine that! if you need to put your boots on to take the dog out, even if we're in the month of May. What crazy weather: it's raining cats and dogs you."
3 "Here in San Martino, it seems like a deluge. I feel like Noah. Only I don't have an ark."
4 Communion and Liberation (CL) is an Italian Catholic movement, founded by the priest Luigi Giussani in 1954 in the Milanese student environment, initially as a branch of Catholic Action. It is characterized by placing the message of the Christian faith as the foundation of every aspect of life.
5 Istituto Italiano di Psicoanalisi di Gruppo.
6 This is the last verse (v.142) of the XXVI Canto dell'Inferno of Dante Alighieri's Divine Comedy.

Chapter 2

Clinical diary of a psychoanalyst in the disease

Round trip journey[1]

Pietro Roberto Goisis

The disease

Like millions of other people in Italy and the world (the actual numbers will never be known), I was infected with SARS-CoV-2 and I became seriously ill. I was then hospitalized for almost two weeks in a sub-intensive care ward. Lucky for me, in the end I was clinically cured, even though this adventure has remained permanently imprinted on me, and I imagine it will never go away.

And I keep talking and writing about it, as I have done since the beginning of the pandemic.

Every day, millions more people get sick, are treated, and recover or die of other diseases. What's so different about my story? Is it really necessary to make such a big deal about it? Perhaps I am exaggerating? I often ask myself this. I haven't found an answer.

Some say it is an epic, one-of-a-kind event, because it has potentially affected everyone, and it is everywhere. This is because we are hyper-connected and alerted in real time about what is happening everywhere in the world (although it is not clear why the events in Wuhan, China, did not give us proper notice in terms of timing ...). Perhaps it was the very type of this disease, which was rather democratic and egalitarian in terms of its transmission, leaving us powerless in the face of its advance and spread, that has led to this collective involvement, in addition to the mystery over its characteristics and ignorance of its symptoms, and especially its treatment. Every day, doctors, virologists, scientists and real or presumed experts argue about the disease's characteristics. We are all being confronted with a disturbing feeling of the unknown, a condition to which we are no longer accustomed, which is difficult to accept and handle. Moreover, when a disease explodes and spreads to emergency rooms, hospitals and skilled nursing facilities, which are entities that should, by definition, protect and treat us, perhaps then we have truly found ourselves living in an upside-down world that we need to deal with, think about and write about.[2] An explosive trauma like this can also be treated through stories, personal accounts and recounting individual experiences.

DOI: 10.4324/9781003198734-3

Writing is a multifaceted endeavour. Anyone who has made an attempt to write knows how important and powerful it is.

Andrea Bocconi, who is a psychologist and writer and trains people to write autobiographies, described some of writing's functions. First and foremost, it is cathartic. It is also therapeutic ("it allows you to put things at an arm's length distance" and remove yourself from them). It lets you discover things for yourself and do research. It provides perspective, allowing you to see trends and patterns. It's a diversion and a fun pastime. It promotes an internal dialogue resulting from a phase shift that occurs when rereading what you've written. It provides meaning. And it is transcendent (what we write goes beyond what we know about ourselves). This was also the case for me.

To write is to tell a story. To narrate is to expose yourself. Which is exactly what they have always told psychoanalysts not to do.

So, it is worth explaining why I did it and am still doing it. Those fragments of experiences that were etched in my mind moment by moment, gradually became a piece of writing, the first draft of which was finished about a week after leaving the hospital. It was intended mainly for me. And later for our friends, family members and those who had been close to us during the illness.

Everyone was touched by reading a first-hand story of the experience.

One person in particular, Davide, a versatile artist whom I respect greatly, phoned me: "It's great, I immediately read it yesterday evening. I had a hard time sleeping, and it's all your fault. But you can't just keep it for yourself or for us. You have to share it and publish it in a few newspapers!" It seemed to be such an authentic, heartfelt appeal that I overcame my reluctance and listened to him. So, with the help of him and some other friends (Iaia, Marco and Ingrid), we settled on *il venerdì* in Italy, the Nanovic Institute for European Studies at the University of Notre Dame in the United States, and on this piece as well as others in the future, I imagine. This will be therapy for me and others and will provide a service for all of us.

The COVID soundtrack

Music, which meant so much to me during my hospitalization, was a way to celebrate healing in American hospitals. So, whenever a patient was discharged, a song played from the speakers. It was a secular way to celebrate, as opposed to the death knell banned in Bergamo during the hardest, most dramatic moments of the pandemic. The pieces selected ranged from "Here Comes the Sun" by the Beatles, "Don't Stop Believin'" by Journey, U2's "A Beautiful Day" and Queen's "We Are the Champions". Also popular were "Rocky", Rachel Platten's "Fight Song", Judy Garland's "Somewhere Over the Rainbow", Andre Day's "Rise Up" and "Eye of the Tiger" by Survivor. But often the hospital asked the patient if he or she had a preference. It's no surprise that in New York one of the most popular hymns among cured patients was "Empire State of Mind" by Alicia Keys and Jay-Z. Perhaps more than any other song, this piece was emblematic of the city and its vitality in the pre-Covid-19 period. It was an anthem of hope that was tattooed on anyone who had skin in the game.

This was yet another moving sign of the collective, supportive involvement of those who took care of us.

I, too, had my own playlist, not just for my discharge, but for the entire hospital period. Lots of songs and sounds got etched in my mind. But the memory of the person, Arialdo, who provided them during my hospitalization is even more prominent than the music itself. This is a very dear friend who was very close to me; I asked him to send me some musical accompaniment because I truly needed it. I received a playlist he put together called "RoGo, short for "Go Roberto", which includes several different musical genres with lots of variety. He also sent me links to fragments of rare concerts found on YouTube. I made another playlist on Spotify, which was relaxing music by Mozart as well as Bach's harpsichord variations. During my hospitalization I finished reading *Disturbance* by Philippe Lançon, the Charlie Hebdo journalist who survived the massacre in 2015; in the book he recounts his hospital experience, with months and months of waiting, surgeries and convalescence during which Mozart and Bach were always by his side. I didn't know their music well. It was the second playlist of my journey. If I had been able to choose a song that I would have liked to hear when I was leaving, I would have certainly chosen a piece by Ivano Fossati such as "There's Time". It would have been a nice, quiet departure.

A doctor, a psychiatrist, a psychoanalyst … and others

This pandemic has changed many of our guiding principles and habits.

In our work every gesture has a specific content and symbolism. How we open a door, how we greet people when they come in and leave, where we put our hands during sessions, what we do about cuticles around our nails, how we cough and sneeze, how far away we are (who ever thought of measuring it up until now?).

We are used to confronting our thoughts during a session: some are unpleasant, while others are beautiful. We generally attribute them to those talking to us who "put the thoughts in our heads". The pandemic has forced us to face our emotions. Our fears have surfaced: Now we have to worry about age. They tell us, "The elderly over age 65 must stay at home!" How dare they! Which elderly people? Can we work? Can we choose not to work? Where do we draw the line between being responsible and irresponsible, between ethics and sacrifice?

Following the initial precautionary guidelines, the Government Decrees of 8 March 2020 further transformed our work. While initially the proposal to meet others with proper physical distancing was common sense, we were now required to close our offices completely. And we now had to invent or find other ways of meeting and making contact like emails, WhatsApp, FaceTime, Skype and Zoom. What will be next?

What's left of psychoanalysis in all this, what happened to our identity?

The watchword is "to help people", any time, anyway.

It was almost a diagnostic principle in certain respects, because we work by observing what happens to us and to the people we meet. I got very worried when I thought, during this widespread, natural, physiological disaster, what would happen to people who are already stressed on a daily basis over what might happen to them in terms of health. Like me, every other psychoanalyst probably wondered how patients with hypochondriac tendencies would react. This was a very serious thought. I have a habit of discussing things currently happening to us with my patients. I discussed the following issue with one patient: for months he was overcome by the fear of having a specific disorder, that something terrible could happen to him, and over what his symptoms and pain could mean. Suddenly he says: "Doctor, I am not afraid of this virus." And after thinking about it, he adds: "You know, we are on alert every day, so maybe we're more used to managing these alerts than anyone else."

This is how we were able to make sense of this. We hypothesized that the "system" went haywire because it was not prepared to handle an emergency. On the other hand, a hypochondriac is well trained, ready and accustomed to managing this type of situation. And he watches others who get agitated as if they were aliens from another planet.

Instead, I was confident that, with certain exceptions, other patients would "capably" address the moment we were experiencing, and that is what happened, at least among those I met. This has surfaced in the issues discussed, in moods, in emotions shown, and in the behaviours reported despite fluctuations along the spectrum of feelings between minimization and apprehension. In short, I think I can say that they have fared better than most of our fellow citizens. Obviously, the psychological work being done and the ability to rely on a space and someone to talk to were fundamental. This was confirmed by a friendly, smart patient who wrote to me:

> *Those of us who are psychologically unstable can endure. This is because right now we are the ones with more tools, and because we have been training for a long time to resolve our issues.*

It is extremely difficult to summarize the number of changes implemented including emergency-related aspects, individual precautions, health tips and government decrees. This is partly because in just a few weeks the overall scenario has changed at a pace that is sometimes faster than our own ability to adapt, and perhaps even faster than the virus itself.

Whenever individuals have shown flexibility in terms of habits, fears and rigidities, the therapeutic relationship has definitely benefited.

I have shared every decision with my patients from the very beginning. Nearly all of them appreciated this decision and opted for remote meetings. A few others preferred to discontinue therapy and try to get along on their own by postponing the resumption of working together until the end of the crisis.

Hand sanitizers and handwashing have appeared in doctors' offices, and managing distances is no longer just keeping the "right distance", but is measured in metres and centimetres. We have had to deal with giving up fundamental aspects of our way of spending time with others, such as shaking hands at the beginning or end of a session, as well as every spontaneous gesture that was customary for us or our patients. One example of this is a young teenager who, at the end of every session found an unexpected way to say good-bye and thank me: once with a pat on my shoulder, another time "high-fiving" me, and sometimes giving me a strong hug. All of this is subject to change.

On 9 March 2020 my office closed. I could now only do online sessions. It was the law.

Omnipotence and invulnerability

I was worried about my family, other people, my patients and the world in general. But not about me.

How should we define this? It's omnipotence and, I would add, invulnerability. The feeling that most everything can be resolved, and everything can be cured. We feel free of weaknesses and fragility. Of course, I speak for myself, because "I" felt invulnerable, despite alerts, warnings, family advice and everything else. I was very, very careful, however, because I cared about protecting others, and therefore my attention was focused on what could happen to other people and my patients, and to my family. I was one of the first to implement precautionary procedures in my office such as no longer shaking hands, sanitizing and maintaining distances and all the various other things that could be done, but I thought nothing would ever happen to me. I do not know if this attitude is cultural, generational or because I am a man, or if it is part of my profession, or only and exclusively my issue. But during the first two days I still passed through two customs checks and four airports, and I went on two flights, and this was already after the red zone declaration and lockdown of Codogno and Lodi. I was convinced that I would be invincible.

I'm someone who never gets sick, doesn't skip a day of work, and usually doesn't catch a cold. Every year I get the flu vaccination specifically because I am at a vulnerable age, and I see many people every day, but I really thought nothing would happen to me. I cannot exactly say what accounts for this attitude. I thought a lot about this later, and I'm still thinking about it. I felt it was somewhat related to the fantasy that we believe we control and run everything with technology or our minds. This is an enormous illusion, of course, but it was very powerful at the time. And I feel many people continue

Clinical diary of a psychoanalyst in the disease   73

to feel this way, including several colleagues. They believe, incorrectly, that a healthy mind, and good and effective psychoanalysis can protect us from diseases and infections. I have never explicitly believed such a tall tale as this with no scientific basis. I fear, implicitly, that I have lived by this lie in some way. This is certainly one of the things that has changed and will continue to change in me.

How it all began: chronicle of my pre-pandemic experience

It is Sunday, 1 March. I am returning from a wonderful weekend spent in London visiting my daughter who had just given birth, so I had a new granddaughter to meet whom I had only seen in photos. I'm happy to be back, but sorry that I won't be able to see them again for a while, and I arrive at the airport. In London everything seemed normal, as if nothing had happened and nothing was happening. It seemed like no one was wearing a mask. I land at Malpensa, and I'm immediately aware of the change, because at the back of the arrivals area I see masked Red Cross staff with infra-red pointers taking body temperatures. I'm not wearing a mask, of course, because nothing will ever happen to me, as I said earlier ...

I work in the office on Monday, but I feel very tired. In fact, that morning I don't hear the alarm clock, which is something else that is unthinkable in my standard behaviour. I miraculously wake up a few minutes before the appointment with my first patient; I manage to dress quickly, and I rush into the office and make it to the appointment. I am amazed and say to myself: "Wow, what a weekend with all the emotions ... I did it!". I spend the day experiencing some fatigue and chills. "It's odd – I think –. the temperature in the office is generally fine." In the evening I get out the thermometer. I have a little fever.

"I must be a little tired", I say again, naturally. A perfect textbook case of denial.

The next day I work again. In the evening I take my temperature again: just a mild fever, a few degrees, but I feel extremely tired. So, as a good citizen, I call the regional number for assistance and information. They answer immediately, the phone rang on their end maybe three times. A very nice young woman answers.

"Please don't worry", she says, "it's just a little fever. Call your primary care physician tomorrow, but with a temperature of 99.5 there is no problem ..."

I say: "But is there a risk that ...?"
"No, please don't worry."
I insist: "Should I call back if ...?"
"No, just call your primary care physician."
The next morning, I call my primary care physician who repeats the same things to me.

> "Do you have any complaints?"
>
> "Yes, fatigue."
>
> "Do you have a cough?"
>
> "No, no cough."
>
> "Are you having trouble breathing?"
>
> "No."
>
> "Any other complaints?"
>
> "Intestinal problems."
>
> "Oh, OK, but that isn't relevant."

This was early March. Ignorance of the Covid virus was rampant. I'm not mad at anyone, yet.

"Take some paracetamol."

And so, I kept on going Tuesday, Wednesday, Thursday.

My wife, who was still far away helping our daughter and granddaughter, was very worried. I was supposed to go see them, but I repeated my promise that if I had a fever I would not get on a plane. Which was the case. Friday I didn't work, I stay quietly at home and then comes Saturday.

I am slumped over and exhausted. The only possible refuge is sinking into the bed. I sleep endlessly.

I hardly eat a thing. The idea of food is disgusting. I'm not interested.

My wife realizes that things are not good. So, she decides to return early. She arrives and sees I'm a "mess". But I was still convinced that all I had was just a "little flu". At this point, we decided to get help and support from the primary care physician and other outside experts. We wanted to get a test done. Impossible. A friend, who was also a primary care physician, convinces us to start a round of antibiotics that I begin on Sunday, with no result. On Monday morning they have me get a chest x-ray. And some lab tests. Once again, we made these decisions independently and carried them out in the private sector because the public health system was unfortunately unable to help, the primary care physician didn't make house calls, home care was not available, and so on. I get the response very quickly and remember my ridiculous enthusiasm. The data seem to indicate that it is a bacterial pneumonia, and this is one of the paradoxes of the moment. I was happy to have bacterial pneumonia because it meant not having a Covid-related pneumonia. I spend the day almost euphoric. I warn my patients about my illness, and I reassure them that I would recover in a week.

Emergency room

The illusion didn't last long. Even the second antibiotic didn't help. On Tuesday afternoon, 10 March, we called the emergency number, 112, and finally the home ambulance service was working. At this point, I have the first "real" contact with the disease. Outfitted stretcher bearers arrive who look like they're dressed for a film about bacteriological warfare. Ambulance workers have a very difficult job. They are usually kind people, and often friendly. The meeting with them also looks like it will be fun. I was worried about what could happen to my patients in my absence, on the days when I couldn't see them.

"Doctor, your patients need you to be alive!" They are smart, indispensable, meticulous and effective.

I recall that the emergency room is a no man's land. There's a feeling of loneliness and isolation. When I make the curve to go where I need to sit and wait I realize there are some problems. Not all the chairs can be used. I see some patients who are very sick, and older patients who are probably in the terminal phase. I'm very scared. The emergency room is filled with a number of people facing major challenges in their lives. We may differ by skin colour, national origin, social conditions, religion and ideals, but now I am one of them. The wait seems endless, which is typical of the emergency room. And the staff is in a heightened state of alarm. They were walking around very alarmed and restless but were very professional. I met with an extraordinary young doctor who was extremely kind and very professional but overwhelmed by bureaucracy. He impressed me because after the test he told me: "Be patient, because the testing procedure is nothing compared to the endless paperwork I have to fill out and the forms I have to send for doing this test."

Then a long and exhausting wait begins. On the other hand, I was fine, I was a code green. It's my turn, but it was well past one in the morning when I was already thinking about leaving. They do an initial examination. When the results arrive – they finally even did a test, but it would take a day to get results – the doctor tells me: "We don't know if it is bacterial pneumonia. Whether it is or not, there is definitely serious respiratory failure. You meet certain parameters that force us to admit you." This is when the madness begins. Overtaken by the fear of immediate hospitalization, I manage to have them send me home, and I check myself out. I force my wife, whom I had not informed of my self-discharge, to come pick me up in the middle of the night. When she sees me outside staggering with the bag I had brought for a possible hospital stay, she is obviously frightened. But she doesn't say a word. I will always thank her for her silence that evening. She was able to keep quiet because she decided that in any case the next day she would have me hospitalized by hook or by crook. I too wanted to be hospitalized. I just wanted to choose the place and when to do it. This was a bit of a crazy fantasy, as if I were selecting a resort hotel on the internet.

The next morning, another ambulance, and another trip to the emergency room. This time it was code yellow with the sirens blaring. It was a very short wait. At this point, it was as if I were home. There were additional detailed examinations and immediate hospitalization in a ward. It was a double room, but for single use, of course. I was still waiting for the results of the swab test. The treatment continues, I am still not feeling well, but they give me oxygen that helps me a lot. At that time, I was still convinced that I didn't have the Covid virus, but they did tests for every possible systemic or pulmonary infection, so at some point I feared I had a blood infection, one of those that is fatal or requires blood washings. I don't know how I spent the day while waiting. The next morning, I get the test result: POSITIVE. On the one hand, I was relieved, but I was also terrified. They take me to the appropriate hospital, Luigi Sacco Hospital; I'm lucky, I keep thinking. I take all my stuff with me in the ambulance, because they scared me on the first day saying they would burn all my infected clothes. That was the first contact with the disease and the shame of being sick, which is the subject I cover next.

Shame

The most unpleasant impact at Fatebenefratelli Hospital was when a nurse who had just left my room told her colleagues: "I'm dirty." She meant that she had been in contact with me. The thought was simple: If she is dirty, so am I. "Dirty" makes sense in nursing jargon, but it is much more unpleasant than "infected". It creates a sense of blame for getting dirty and the resulting shame. Feeling dirty, and therefore sick, I felt like I was dangerous and ashamed to be sick. So, I did something that I only later realized. When I was told about the positive test result, I did not notify my patients. I initially informed them I had "bacterial" pneumonia. Then I said I was hospitalized for "a widespread lung infection". I could not bring myself to say: "I have tested positive for Covid." And obviously this also put my patients at risk since they had been close to me the prior week. Fortunately, no one has become ill. But it was only later that I realized this. Someone got angry, and rightly so, and said to me: "Really, doctor ...." She was right. In part it was due to the fact that I was not well, and I was not very lucid, but, to be clear, to tell someone I was Covid positive also gave me the feeling that I was a plague-spreader. And we all know what happens to plague-spreaders.

Journey to hell

When determining what was happening in the gradual worsening of my clinical condition, I had the feeling of the inevitable, like a staircase that I started to go down, an escalator that I could not stop on which I was stuck, preventing me from doing anything. I couldn't go back up. I just had to stay there and go down. Each trip was a mixture of profound anxiety, because I understood that I was going ever lower, and at the same time, a curious feeling of relief because I felt that in any case, when it was determined what was happening to me, I was hoping and thinking that others could do something about this problem and help me take care of it. This gives you an idea of the mix of feelings I experienced.

Fear

Was I afraid? This is one of the three questions I most frequently ask myself. I usually answer that I was scared, more than experiencing fear. This happened while I was waiting to know what I had. When I found out, it almost completely stopped. I wanted to live, and I felt incredibly sad that I would miss the chance to see other people, experience joys and hopes and make plans. It bothered me to have unfinished business. I think I found my salvation in trying to stay where I was, and not venturing into inevitable thoughts of death. I tried doing it in any way possible. I focused on details. I desperately focused on particulars, which helped me recognize the people behind the masks and outfits, but it also helped me a lot to stay alive. I concentrated on the details of a change in scenery: while in the ambulance I looked at the sky through the windows, and I realized what street we were on. When I entered the hospital grounds, I followed the route along roads in the park, and when I entered the ward, I looked at where all the staff were, how they were dressed, and what room they put me in. All of this was extremely helpful to me to feel that no matter what, even though I was going down the stairway to hell, I maintained contact with the life I was allowed to live at that moment. This was my way of hoping and attempting not to let this be a one-way trip.

An enlightened psychiatrist, who is a dear friend, told me about his experience working in a sanatorium during the years when people died from tuberculosis. It struck him that none of the patients, not even the most religious, had the desire to die, and could not resign themselves to this fate. He realized that almost all of them were making the same desperate attempt I was making to stay connected with the world and existence by establishing a link with the minutiae and minor events of daily hospital life.

Healing through connections

First of all, healing would require me to rely on others. And relying on someone means trusting them.

Healing also meant the need to establish human connections with all the people I met, starting with the stretcher bearer in the ambulance, to the time when I asked the emergency medical doctor what he wanted to do as a young man. This continued every time I met someone in the ward, and when they put me in an isolated room, where, however, I no longer had the feeling of being dirty. There was great respect for our condition and care in that environment. They asked us to adhere to safety procedures, but I pointed out that they were already used to moving around in contact with us infected patients. However, I tried to maintain a connection with every person entering the room, whether it was a doctor, a nurse or cleaning staff. I tried to find a few words, take an interest in their mannerisms or things, or ask a personal question. This created a relationship dynamic which was vital for me, but I

"Bubble" helmet (helmet-based ventilation)

This was another one of my "healing friends".

After telling me, and perhaps even making me realize, that I was in pretty bad shape, the doctors immediately added, "But there is a solution, in addition to all the treatments we will try and ultimately use. We would like to use the 'helmet'. It works very well and is showing promising results." I had no idea what it was. The only helmets I knew about were motorcycle helmets and the helmet-type hair dryers used by women's hairdressers. The helmet arrived a few minutes later, maybe an hour after being admitted, and they put it on me. I wore it for up to 20 hours a day, for five days. There are several models, proudly produced in the "tech valley" between Bologna and Modena according to a friend from Bologna. This thought gave me a certain degree of comfort. The helmet is a sort of mix between a diving suit helmet and a plastic ball, which is transparent fortunately, and they obviously put it on your head. It is connected to an oxygen concentrator, and sits on your neck, and a flexible component, which at first seemed strange to me, is used to pump in air under high pressure. So, the helmet rests directly on the skin of your neck, creating a vacuum effect, so to speak, because in reality you're inside an air turbine, with an extremely high concentration of oxygen.

It has two, and perhaps even three, major disadvantages.

Your head is enclosed in a very tight space. Luckily, I'm not claustrophobic, but I know some people had to be sedated to put up with wearing the helmet.

The air circulates in the helmet and, as long as your fever is high, it runs at unbearable temperatures, making you dizzy from the heat.

Finally, the noise from the high-pressure air entering the helmet is excruciating, like the cabin of a plane with no sound insulation, a truly unbearable noise. All of this further accentuates the separation, loneliness and isolation from the outside world. My communication with that world was on sheets of paper. The nurses would come and write something on a piece of paper. I yelled in an attempt to get them to hear me, but I was never sure if they did. Sometimes they would get close and scream something near my ears further exacerbating an already tense relationship.

Another problem was the number of hours spent in the helmet. It is a helmet in every sense of the word, meaning it is round and bulky making sleeping or even resting nearly impossible. It makes a truly terrifying noise. I don't know if I was the first person to think of this, but I had an idea that

Clinical diary of a psychoanalyst in the disease   79

maybe one solution would be to use some sort of earplugs. At first they made me a set of cotton earplugs, but later I got them in my daily supply packages that arrived from home. Then I came up with the idea of having my headphones brought in to listen to music.

Thankfully, this allowed me to raise the volume of the sound, creating a sort of tolerance for this head-splitting noise. Among the many crazy thoughts I had at that time was that even if I managed to survive, I might never work again. My work is based on listening. "I will go deaf", I thought. Luckily, this did not happen, and I can still hear people.

But at that time crazy thoughts really took hold; some were a little foolish, some drifted to the future and the hope to live, and some to the present, and what was happening to me at that moment. I continued to focus on details, including protecting myself from excessive noise or creating a sound that was actually pleasant. These were long, arduous journeys inside this noisy plane in which I found myself remaining still but travelling long distances with my mind and thoughts.

My thoughts

There were frightening and crazy thoughts, but also crucial reflections, especially at night. It was difficult to sleep in the helmet: I seemed to be blessed on one side and cursed on the other. Mercifully, there were moments of sanity sprinkled among the evil and crazy thoughts. One was that if I did indeed manage to survive, I wanted to write something about what was happening to me. My writing took the form of making short notes wherever I could, on pieces of paper, the iPad or a computer. I left behind tracks in the form of words, sort of like Tom Thumb leaving behind breadcrumbs.

It seems that I developed quite a unique reputation in the ward, when they discovered that, even while inside the helmet, sitting up straight in the bed, I was writing with a Mac on my lap. Those tracks were more a connection with my mind than the outside world, and they stayed untouched on my computer for 15–20 days. I gradually felt the desire to return to life and re-establish contacts as I started to connect with the outside world, friends and family. But the strongest urge to write came one day from a young doctor, who started to leave the room after visiting, updating and greeting us, and then stopped, turned back and suddenly said to me, "After you leave, you'll have to send us what you're writing!"

His words really got to me. A very perspicacious young man!

Holding on

At the low points, the prevailing sentiment was to fight for something. I never liked using war as a metaphor during my illness and the pandemic, but that was just a personal sensibility. On the other hand, who likes wars? I didn't feel like I had to fight a war; I felt like I had to try to stay alive.

There were no thoughts on what had happened, and there were no regrets, just a focus on the moment and the concern that something could go wrong. I never really feared I would die at that time. Many have asked me about this. It may seem strange, because in actuality, according to the doctors I got very close, but I never really had a fear of dying. I was more afraid of losing something, which is perhaps similar, but it was really about losing my integrity, for example. This was very important to me. I am often told that I look young for my age. Even when I arrived at the hospital, someone said I looked younger than my actual age. I immediately thought, "Let's hope that this virus doesn't overwhelm me, and cause me to suddenly catch up with my age …".

I held on tight to this thought.

The alien

Having this infection is like having an alien inside you who won't let you go and puts up a formidable fight. I realized very quickly that this monster had affected me far more than I realized, and more than clinical tests showed: It had attacked every part of me. First it weakened my muscles and joints, then a fever and intestinal problems came up (at Sacco Hospital, they already knew this was a typical symptom), high blood pressure and heart problems, and finally I had problems with my lungs, which were "wet", as they told me, and therefore I could not breathe. And I was no longer able to feed myself. Then my skin was assaulted with dryness, itching and peeling. And my fingernails came next: two fingernails suddenly started retracting as if they were going away. Problems in my liver and kidneys followed that. Lastly, I was consumed by weakness and unable to move. Being immobile, the feeling of losing my strength was overwhelming.

In fact, when the alien finally left, another key aspect I felt was the need to take better care of myself. Despite my best intentions, I had really neglected this.

Self-care

While I was ill it was impossible to take care of myself in any way. My beard grew, and my hair was dirty and dishevelled. Washing was not possible, even though the nurses tried to give me a hand. It was essential to be able to start taking care of myself again as soon as I felt a little better, so I needed to use a little ingenuity. I had to shave and wash my hair in a sink, because the bathroom had no shower, and I wanted to get up and start moving my muscles a bit. It even helped just to look out the window and feel the warmth of the heart-rending March sun. I started to realize that I needed to actively focus on what I was made of, my organs and body parts and endeavour to care for them and keep them healthy even before dealing with my mind, desires or dreams. Looking again at details, I needed to pay more attention to the little things, like changing a vest, putting on fresh pyjamas and tasting food again, including what was served in the hospital or special food brought from home.

When my body started to show signs of improvement, my mind was quick to follow, and when it got better, so did my body. In Italy, we always wonder which came first, the chicken or the egg. This question deserves an answer, but at the same time, it emphasizes the fact that the mind and body are closely connected. Even in the West we see a close link between mind and body.

Mindfulness

For several years I have taken an interest in certain disciplines aimed at self-care, reducing stress, improving mental functioning, relaxation and well-being in a broad sense. Practising mindfulness on a daily or as-needed basis, addresses these needs.

During my hospitalization, when breathing was so heavily compromised, it seemed that every breath was extremely precious and worth improving, even if it was not always possible.

Above all, the practice helped me to focus on the awareness of my presence in what was happening, at every moment in my life, providing me with a good sense of serenity. I didn't care if the bed was comfortable or uncomfortable, or if the sheets were soft or stiff. I was there and had no choice in the matter. Complaining would have been pointless, or perhaps even a further irritant.

This was also true of the equally conscious acceptance of events and medical procedures. This attitude served me well the dozens of times blood samples were taken from my veins and arteries. Just let the needles go in, I said to myself each time. This almost always worked!

Loneliness

I have never been a big fan of phones and various other devices, but in this situation, I could not have been happier to have a phone and iPad. I also had my computer brought in. These tools were my connection with the world, my family and friends. They also served as a way to maintain contact with my patients as things improved. And these contacts led to small requests and short messages. There were countless pleasant memories: a friend who sent a playlist on Spotify, patients who wrote get-well cards, and family members who sent emoticons.

When things got bad, it was difficult to even think of sending or looking at a message, but the night when they proposed using an emergency treatment, I was happy to do so. However, I realized that if they were suggesting something to me at night, there was a serious problem, so I resorted to the internet. I typed what they told me ("it's a drug we use in rheumatoid arthritis"), and started reading about what it was, its benefits and its side effects. At that point, I turned off the computer and told myself to just let them do what they wanted. I then sent a message to my wife who was at home and much more worried than I was: "They want to try a new therapy on me and say it could help a lot." We exchanged messages that night, which I think helped her, because she knew that they were doing something for me, but also helped me to send off a sort of message in a bottle, like a castaway on a desert island. In actuality, this realization came only later: Covid patients are LONELY. This is necessarily true due to the characteristics and contagious nature of the disease. If you then spend hours in a helmet or end up in intensive care, loneliness becomes sensory deprivation. It's really like being in another world.

Crying

My daughter lives in London. On the afternoon of Thursday, 19 March, which is Father's Day in Italy, she called me for a little chat. I was already feeling better, I was calmer, and I was happy to chat. When the conversation ended, I gave a huge sigh of relief and – it's about to happen again even now as I recall the event and write about it – I burst into uncontrollable tears and sobbing. Fortunately, my roommate was inside his bubble helmet, and I was able to give ample space to the emotions that had built up for far too many days.

My son, who was in charge of providing daily supplies of clean linens and basic necessities that I could not find, touched me when he sent photos of the outside of the building where my ward is located, and of the lush greenery growing uncontrollably in the hospital park.

Crying is different. Being able to cry was definitely a sign that I was actually going to make it. Others would experience the same feelings nearly always accompanied by emotions and tears in their eyes.

I am not ashamed of this; in fact, I'm happy to recall my crying episodes and talk about them with pride.

My guardian angels

Helpful people have been there for me for various situations in my life. Someone I had treated several years ago, and who came to see me for an office visit somewhat later, found out I had been hospitalized and tried to find out where I was. When she discovered where I was she said, "Oh, you're at Sacco Hospital. My sister and brother-in-law work there, maybe they can give you a hand." I then told her with no reservation, "Do whatever you want". Over time she got quite close to me, and sent a message wishing me a good morning every day along with information on my health and so on. It was nice to have her there. I am not used to hearing from my patients every day, including by text message, but having her there was very important to me. This curious coincidence (although nothing really happens by chance …) provided me with a sort of local spy inside the ward. There really was no need, because they were all very dear and sensitive, which was a very important part of the care. But having this support made me feel a little more protected, like someone was watching out for me.

Thanks, Anna.

My medical team

The relationship I had with doctors was nothing short of extraordinary. I got the impression that as happy as I was to get better, they were equally eager to make sure all of us got better. Although they certainly didn't want to lose us from the standpoint of a medical failure, they also didn't want to see any human beings die. Thus, I truly felt that my doctors were amazing cheerleaders.

The nurse at Fatebenefratelli Hospital, who made the comment about being "dirty", was certainly more frightened than I was. At Sacco Hospital, the atmosphere was totally different, because it was a ward dedicated solely to Covid, so they really knew what they were doing. They were equipped with every possible protection and knew how to protect themselves. In addition to personal and group attitudes, I was impressed by their expertise, not to mention their caring and kindness. They left me with endless experiences to remember and relate.

One day, when my temperature was taken for the umpteenth time, and was finally normal, a doctor attempted to give me a high five as if I had scored a three-point shot at the decisive moment at the end of a basketball game. I was in my helmet. I said to myself, "She must be crazy, I'm infected and she's giving me a high five?" Another doctor said, "We are cheering for you and hope everything turns out OK. It's like when an Italian athlete wins a medal at the Olympics and I break out crying." She was definitely getting emotional. Another doctor drew a heart in the air with her fingers when they recorded another positive parameter as if she had scored a goal at San Siro stadium and wanted to signal her fiancé or mother in the stands. Those who read my article, wrote to me, "Thank you, you have given me a smile that makes my face glow" or "it was nice to have you as a patient". In short, these were experiences that touched me deeply and made me feel that I was not alone in my daily hospital life. They certainly went well beyond the scope of their medical duties and performed an act of kindness with a truly human touch.

These actions initiated a process of mutual recognition. For others, facial gestures were obscured by masks, glasses, headphones, screens, coats and other personal equipment that were so effective that during my entire hospitalization I was not able to associate a name, job or position with any of the healthcare workers who came in my room.

I never felt like I was just a number or a bed. They always treated me like a person, with a first and last name.

And this was extremely important.

Care and treatment

I often find myself wondering what cured me, and what specific therapies were a part of my treatment. I know that they did, and gave me everything they thought was useful based on data being collected around the world. When I was still going through one of the riskiest periods, a nurse came in and said, "We want to use an experimental therapy on you, and we want to do it now". I was inside my bubble helmet and didn't understand what she was suggesting, so she wrote it on a piece of paper: It's an IV drip, and will last – as I read it – 24 hours. With a totally amazed look on my face, I yelled inside the helmet, "24 hours?" "No, I made a mistake. It lasts two and a half hours". "OK", I said, "do whatever you want to me!"

I would have even agreed to magic if they had told me it would help.

However, in one of my last acts in the hospital, as a part of the plain-spoken relationships established with all staff, I teased the "poor" speciality registrar who was taking my last arterial blood draw (EGA). "Doctor, leaving scientific claims aside, can you tell me, as a percentage breakdown, to what extent the following aspects were beneficial for my recovery: your expertise, treatments used and … dumb luck?" Without even thinking she answered, "30–30–30". I immediately got the impression that she put the emphasis on the third component. She was being kind.

Later on, someone pointed out to me that the total of the percentages did not add up to 100 as expected.

If I can write off my DNA, health conditions, good nutrition and always taking the right path at every crucial crossroads to nothing more than "dumb luck", then perhaps the remaining 10 per cent is something even more difficult to define. Giancarlo Zapparoli, one of my mentors, would have called it resilience, a term that is now misused somewhat, which he was already using clinically in the 1990s. To me it seemed to be something vague, imprecise, elusive, but powerful and decisive such as inner strength, trust in my resources, mental stamina, a love for life and the desire to continue to live it. It was that same reasonable and powerful faith in someone else's capabilities that I put into practice in my work, and that my patients acknowledge, for which they seem to be grateful.

In comments in a Facebook post that fully told my story, a Brazilian colleague working in Rome wrote:

> I would like to point out that in addition to dumb luck and the treatment he received, Roberto's recovery was due, in no small part, to his ability to continually practice self-criticism, maintain an inner dialogue, and constantly reflect on his situation, and then later his ability to put into words the painful, life-changing experience he lived through, with an open mind, following various lines of reasoning, from different perspectives, while also examining his emotions and the emotional interaction with others, near and far. Despite the dire situation, his story shows that this was a learning experience not only for him, but for us as well.

Support relationships

While living through the disease, I tried in some way to focus not only on professional considerations, but on human connections as well. I needed to do this to feel like I was living and not just letting myself go. I never forgot that I was a patient first, but one evening, during the night shift, two nurses came in my room, approached my bed and said, "Doctor, we have something serious we need to talk about". It was possible that they had something very unpleasant to say about me, but I realized that the conversation was going in another direction. So, I said to myself: OK, I'm listening. They moved closer to the bed and said, "We nurses need help: we are exhausted, worn out, and when we go home, all we want to do is sleep, and we're worried that we will give the virus to our family members, children, and so on. In fact, we fall asleep immediately, but suddenly wake up in the middle of the night with a vision of our patients' eyes – the same you have – inside the helmets and we can no longer go back to sleep". On the one hand, I realized how frightening we were as patients, and how we were capable of scaring others. But I also realized that they were asking me for professional assistance, which made me think that I must be getting better. I felt proud and happy, and started to say, "I see, this is significant: you get way too involved. You have to try to put yourselves in the shoes of others, but then stay true to yourselves." "No, no, no", they said, "we know all this very well, we want something to sleep." And then the psychoanalyst in me immediately changed register, and I became a psychiatrist, doctor and a person with good common sense. "OK, all right, give me an email address, and I'll send you details with precise instructions. However, I will also tell you right now. There are various ways to help you: A starting point would be to take some high-quality melatonin, then an anxiety-reducing medication to help you sleep a little better, and then there are some other tools. First, you need to stop thinking when this happens. Then imagine a red button, like an emergency button to disconnect the power. When these thoughts begin to swirl in your head, think of this button, picture it being very big, then press it to turn off your thoughts, and see if that works. Then, if need be, there are other things you can do, which we can take a look at later."

They all left happy, and then received my mail. Two days later they appeared at the door of my room and said, "Doctor, it worked! We are sleeping very well, the melatonin is incredible, and in addition, the red button works wonderfully." When he read this story, a patient of mine said, "Doctor, you need to patent this advice to use the red button. You really have to patent the button!"

How did you get it?

This was definitely the most common question I was asked. Some people reached their own conclusions.

That's fine. I realize why people are so curious about the specifics: If they know how you got infected, maybe they can prevent it from happening to them. This whole episode has made me much more patient with human needs and requirements. Everyone has their own particular weaknesses and vulnerabilities. I accept these.

But I really don't know how to respond to this question. In fact, I'm just not interested. I have never wondered about this, and I have never tried to trace the chain of infection. I may be making a medical mistake by taking this approach, and I'm sorry if that is the case. In fact, from the very beginning, from the moment I discovered I was sick, my emotional position was to focus on the disease. I knew I had it, and now I had to make sure that they treated it, and that I let them treat me. What would have changed if I had known how, when and from whom I got it? Would it have helped somehow? Would it be useful now?

An image comes to mind from a film: *The Bridge of Spies.*

The plot goes something like this. It takes place in the post-war era during the Cold War. After painstaking investigations, the CIA arrests a Russian citizen living in the United States on charges of being a spy. The man, a diminutive, nondescript, mild-mannered person, displays no reaction to events concerning him. For reasons of fairness and respect for the rights of the defendant, the US government puts a young, brilliant lawyer in charge of his defence who gets emotionally involved in the situation. Without going into the substance of the developments of the whole storyline and its ending, the aspects that came to mind concern the reaction of the alleged spy and the emotional involvement of the lawyer.

On several occasions, the latter asks his client the following question:

"You don't seem alarmed." "Don't you ever worry?"

And the small man, invariably, answers:

"Would it change anything?" "Would it help?"

I consider this reaction, this way of experiencing a very difficult situation, to be an excellent example of mindfulness and awareness, which is similar to how I experienced my illness and getting sick. I should stress that the important thing is to protect ourselves, to try not to get sick, and to take all the precautions to help us avoid infection. We need to be cautious and focused.

What was the role of other patients?

Good question. It definitely is on the mind of anyone who has had the misfortune of being hospitalized, and who has found the support and value of talking to other patients about their illness and hospital stay. However, anyone hospitalized for Covid-19 could never be asked this question since so many were intubated, sedated, in a coma or resuscitated. Each of us afflicted by the disease was forced to be alone, even during our illness. In some cases, this was a good thing, in others, not so much. During my hospital stay, I had only one such encounter, with my travelling companion in the ambulance from the Fatebenefratelli Hospital to Sacco Hospital. He then also became my roommate, and his name was Alberto.

There are times when you prefer to be alone, when solitude provides discretion and tranquillity. I must confess that I too, at the beginning of my hospitalization, would have preferred to have the room to myself. Alberto was at least 15 years younger than me, and he was not nearly as sick based on what doctors had told him from the start. He seemed to be the type of person who liked to complain and make accusations, but I was in no mood for that. He didn't seem very interested in me either.

Then, slowly, and very gradually, hour after hour, and day after day, we started to pay more attention to each other. We shared what was happening to us, our pleasures and concerns, as well as progress made and relapses. We became relentless cheerleaders for each other. We shared fragments of our lives, anecdotes and private thoughts, and discovered common areas of distant acquaintances or places, including some shared interests. Alberto, who was an IT manager for a major pharmaceutical company, managed to achieve a level of confidence with me that often took several years for me to establish with friends. He opened up to me.

We provided great company to each other, especially in the evening after dinner while getting ready to go to sleep. I'm still amazed that I remember that. I don't believe there was a change in my behavioural DNA: I just think that the perception of accidentally and simultaneously ending up on the same lifeboat during a shipwreck led to an unthinkable feeling of closeness and solidarity. And we were truly in the same boat!

Alberto stayed in the hospital one more week than I did, and he was terrified, with good reason, over who he could end up with as a roommate. I got in touch with him remotely and provided support and comfort.

If everything went well, we intended to get together again in the countryside with our families.

After about three months of sharing our mutual stories of convalescing by phone, we did indeed get together. When we met again, after exchanging a nod of approval, we embraced. It was the first human being, other than a family member, who agreed to do this. Since we were both immune, overcoming the disease called for a hug.

The Greek chorus

I soon found out that far from the hospital, but close to my heart, an incalculable multitude of people experienced concerns, fears, hopes, joys and relief along with me and my family. I pictured them as a teeming chorus in a classical Greek drama that supported me and pushed me from behind while clearing the way in front of me. Perhaps I'm not being very scientific, but I know that everyone was a part of my care. I heard from people whom I never met and heard back from others I thought I'd never hear from again.

Obviously, more than anyone, I felt the presence and closeness of my family members, starting with Emma, my beloved 5-year-old granddaughter who lives in London. She and I have a habit of sharing long, amusing video calls. Obviously during my hospitalization, I only had video calls with my wife, Emma's grandmother. Emma is a little "controlling", so one day she left her mother's side with her phone in her hand and asked her grandmother in a low voice: "So what happened to grandfather?"

The hero

A dear colleague and friend of mine called me "his hero".

Others have said that my story chronicles the achievements of a hero.

However, the myth of a hero assumes there is a path. We are heroes on our personal journeys that encompass the events we experience, on the basis of which we grow, change our attitudes and learn to look at life and others in a new way. As in a fairy tale, we have a treasure to find and a dragon to slay. The former represents the identification of the true self, and our talents and attitudes. The latter symbolizes our internal fears and limitations. On the face of it, this is an endless journey, because the discovery of our value, our self, and the deepest meaning of our life is endless. It can take place in stages and degrees throughout the course of our existence, allowing us, when we truly feel "ourselves", to inhabit our kingdom. This may, perhaps, involve changing it a little or a lot from time to time, just as the hero himself transforms and changes.

I don't know if I was a hero. I think I was just very lucky. Maybe even heroes need luck to cope. Rhetorically speaking, the true heroes were the people who helped me directly and those who supported me in more subtle ways. The only heroic thing that I did was to stay in the hospital, endure the situation and keep my vital body parts alive.

If a hero changes when he finishes his journey, I too think I have changed.

I used to feel heroic when I worked 12 hours a day, and when I saw 14 patients a day. And, out of an extreme ethical duty to perform, I always said yes to every request and schedule change and to almost everyone expressing a need. I think the new heroic part I will play, perhaps as a new hero, will now be my ability to say no. I will try to take better care of myself, for example, to take some time between one patient and another, apart from sanitization requirements, and to allow myself breaks when I need to recharge. This might involve taking a few holidays when I need them or taking a few days off without work. My patients will manage, and I can stay in touch with them by email or video. Perhaps the change I've made from having and recovering from the virus is that I try to be less heroic and strive to be nicer to myself.

Coming home

My return home began when they gave me the green light to be discharged. This was not easy to come by, and certainly not taken for granted. First there were promises, then changes, then more changes.

Then there was a test for the final return home.

I had to take a walk in the hallway, an area where we infected patients were not allowed to go. The point of this was to assess my oxygen saturation under stress, and my respiratory condition. I walked about 20 metres until I reached a wall with a giant poster depicting a rainbow and those famous words, "everything will be fine" that some people were actually not so fond of, including, perhaps, myself. There were actually two walks. I did it the first time, and then returned; my saturation was good, but then Marta, the doctor, said, "Do it a second time, but walk faster". I smiled and felt like I was taking university exams: I got a perfect score on the first one, and the second one was a question for extra credit. I was happy to repeat the test, and very satisfied. The saturation was still good, and at this point I got the green light to leave in a few hours.

The first image I have of my departure was my son waiting in the car. The second image, which left a real imprint, was a selfie with him driving and me in the back seat flashing the victory sign. In the foreground were his happy eyes peering over the mask. Someone said that his look and his eyes were how I must have looked when he was born.

I remember the surreal journey, through the empty streets of Milan, which was still much better than the trip there in the ambulance. When I arrived at my doorstep, a friend was waiting for me at a safe distance, because he wanted to give me the pulse oximeter that I would need for monitoring. He threw me the package, and I responded with a sign of enthusiasm.

At last, I was home and reunited with my wife who was waiting for me. We looked like two mimes. To be on the safe side, we obviously could not get close to each other, because I was in quarantine, and we still did not know whether she had contracted the virus or not. I walked in, and in the hallway of our home, we looked intensely at each other from a distance for a long time with open arms, as if we were preparing a long hug in slow motion.

This is how we hugged each other.

On Monday, 23 March 2020, three weeks after my first symptoms, 13 days after my initial hospitalization and 11 days after the diagnosis, I was at home, getting ready to start another period of isolation involving physical rather than social distancing.

Lockdown and quarantine

These two terms have almost the same meaning for me having spent the first two weeks of lockdown in the hospital and the next three in quarantine. I realized the true distinction only when I was told that the second control test came back negative. At that point I became a normal citizen with many limitations and a few possibilities. As a "survivor", I think it is only natural to focus more on the latter than the former. I took pleasure in every moment, every experience, every lunch, every event I could experience. In the first few days I definitely spent more time on the phone than I did in the previous year and was happy to do so. I repeated my story and current status ad infinitum. No question seemed too trivial or tedious. I was happy to take the time to answer all of them, and always had an anecdote to tell.

Like many people, I was able to appreciate that my daily life had taken on a different pace and that I could resume abandoned interests and focus on new ones. Do I dare say that I felt serene?

I knew very well this was brought about by both economic security and social standing, and by the fact that I could do at least some of my job, and would certainly resume all normal routines eventually. I felt truly privileged.

And this was partly due to some significant changes I made in my life. I have now resolved to take breaks between sessions (which I am still doing as a result of Covid); I only have a few sessions a day, and distribute work throughout the week, doing a "little bit every day".

I slipped up a few times, like when I saw my first patients online on the very afternoon I left the hospital. I really must have gone overboard: about a week or two after my recovery, one of my patients, who is generally very discrete and respectful, said to me, "Doctor, do you realize what you looked like in those first few days?" I can't say I disagreed with her, and it would be wrong to ignore her and not learn from her comment.

At the same time, I realized the importance of devoting time to new priorities during the day. I focused on good nutrition, dedicating quality time to family relationships, devoting time to self-care and fitness with physical exercises and online courses almost daily.

And my work would come next.

The Coronavirus has caused many human beings to suffer, fall ill and die, and it has also threatened to "eliminate" psychoanalysis and psychotherapies, by undermining the very ability to continue these practices in a normal, physical setting. To adapt to our new environment, it took care, shrewdness and adaptations aimed, first and foremost, at survival, and then it was necessary to maintain a therapy-oriented system in order to continue to "retain a human touch". This led to the widespread use of online therapies that allowed us to work at home and survive.

Some psychoanalysts have reacted to government restrictions by claiming the right/duty to continue working with a physical presence in their offices. They stood up to the law, government decrees and common sense, and risked their own health and that of their patients. They said they feared, and I would agree, that psychoanalysis would no longer be the same if practised online, and that this transition would be a point of no return and decline of this speciality.

We all need to protect ourselves as best we can and overcome our demons!

Personally, I am happy that I have had the opportunity to continue working safely. This was mainly due to the willingness of my patients to be flexible, but was also the result of an adaptive approach cultivated over the years. I have learned new procedures, lived through intense experiences and studied various strategies. I never thought that an online session was the same as a physical session. They are two different situations that are equally rich and stimulating. We will talk and reflect about this for years.

The trauma

In the months following my hospitalization, I felt that I was having what we can call post-traumatic sequelae. The negative events of our experience seem to become registered in an area of our minds if they are not adequately processed. Then, while seemingly repressed, they act undetected, and subsequently result in post-traumatic pathology. For those who do my job, it is not easy to accept the fact that you show signs of such a disorder. It's not a good state of affairs, and it also has brain-related and neurological implications. However, for some time, I experienced some sort of irritability. I felt very impatient, such as when someone said or did things that I didn't like, or if I felt annoyed or disregarded. I noticed it a little, sometimes in my tone of voice that tended to be a little higher and more distressed when I recounted things, and sometimes I conveyed (and perhaps still convey) a bit of agitation when speaking. Maybe this phenomenon will also be reflected in this book, and in writing and sharing my story that has also played a major role in processing this experience.

Being aware was the first step, and accepting the recommendations of others will follow. Properly dealing with this will be the next and final step.

Covid psychoanalysis from a hospital bed

il venerdì *magazine – No. 1676 – I May 2020*

Finally, the long-awaited day had arrived. My article, which was praised by the editorial staff and with minor editing, would be published in the weekly *la Repubblica* insert, *il venerdì*. I was happy and excited and went to the newspaper stand where I had reserved a few copies. The impact of the printed page was very powerful, almost physical, giving me a sense of fullness and unimaginable satisfaction with tears flowing as I was reading my story, as if it were written by someone else.

At that moment, a number of messages, phone calls, emails and feedback of every kind began coming in, and still is. This was truly unexpected and surprising, and I still have them. I'd like to share a few of the issues that have come up.

- Numerical data. I had started counting the messages received to determine how much work would be needed to individually respond to each of them. I stopped when they topped 500. And they kept on coming for a long time. Even now. The quality of a text is not always proportional to its quantity, but, in my opinion, the sheer volume of responses reflects the impact and power of the story.
- Compassion, emotions, involvement. These feelings are expressed in virtually all the messages received. This direct, open and sincere sharing has really made an impression on me. This was a chronicle from an insider, almost in real time, that allowed readers to literally put themselves in my shoes, as a human being plunged into hell, with the related surprises and experiences of the disease. Readers got so involved that they actually experienced my emotions that were revealed and shared in the story.
- Usefulness. This was perhaps the most widespread sentiment at different levels. The story proved to be useful for various types of people: those who are no longer here and had no voice, those who became ill and couldn't say so, those who are sick and afraid, those who are afraid to get sick, those who did not believe that we could get sick, those who work as medical professionals, and those who live with the latter. It also struck a chord because the tone used in the article was not rhetorical or accusing, and was free of anger or resentment.
- Gratitude. This was one of the most touching forms of praise. And it reinforced my decision to share my story. I felt grateful to those who read my story and wrote me a message. And those who read my article wrote to me to thank me for telling my story.

The very reason I decided to write my diary was to be able to share my experience with the Covid virus.

Notes

1 Based on an interview with *MNEO-Italian Memory* Archive-info@mneo.it/www.mneo.it/Facebook/Instagram
2 In the text I will make several references to an article published in the magazine *il venerdì*, No. 1676–1/5/2020 https://bit.ly/2zO0R2J and https://nanovic.nd.edu/news/surviving-coronavirus/

Conclusions

Pietro Roberto Goisis and Angelo Antonio Moroni

Every time we talked about our experience with the lockdown and Covid-19 we were asked a lot of questions.

- How will we get over it?
- What will we be like after?
- Will we change?

When answering these questions, Roberto always tries to remind everyone that he "only" got sick, and that this does not make him a fortune teller, soothsayer or someone with greater powers. But he does have his own ideas about these issues that are based on the feelings he experienced over the course of these months.

For his part, Angelo has endeavoured to relate and share what he thought, experienced, saw and heard.

It is very likely that this experience, which was so consequential, absorbing and enigmatic, will force us to reconsider our choices and priorities, just as it has already profoundly changed our lives in the past months.

We would like to use this situation to ensure that these problems turn into opportunities.

For example, there are those who have benefited from the lockdown by devoting more time in their lives to their children, spouses and themselves. And this has made it difficult for them to resume a normal life. It has also created a sort of nostalgia for bygone times.

Others are suffering from economic and social uncertainties. Still others are experiencing relationship issues.

And fear is an altogether separate matter: it must be seen on a continuum, where it is absent on one end of the spectrum and serves as a precursor to the phenomena of denial and plotting, and where on the other end, it comes in the form of a constant onslaught leading to phobic states, isolation and avoidance.

Wisdom tells us that the truth lies somewhere in between these extremes (*in medio stat virtus*).

DOI: 10.4324/9781003198734-4

94 Conclusions

Our feeling is that we will have to learn to live with this sly, mysterious adversary for a long time, but science, economics, politics and society are getting ready for the battle ahead. In the end, individual behaviour and decisions will ultimately be the deciding factor that extricates us from this crisis and emergency.

We really don't know if we will change, and what we will be like.

It certainly won't be an automatic process.

Sometimes, we think somewhat pessimistically that it will only improve the lives of those who are already better, but we can't help wondering who decides what and who are better.

And then we go back to the notion of a utopia, to the fantasy of a more just and fairer world.

So, referring to the experiences we covered in this book, we imagine and dream that a day will come when a person:

- is aware of his/her own fragility, without considering it to be a limitation;
- knows how to protect himself/herself and others, while continuing to live;
- takes care of his/her physical and mental health, while respecting that of others;
- trusts the expertise of specialists, and not just Google;
- listens to the words and advice of those who love them;
- knows how to graciously look upon others as allies and not as enemies;
- always stays in touch with himself/herself and with the people s/he meets;
- does not feel ashamed if s/he gets ill, but can accept the disease, and takes care of himself/herself, in the interest of the individual and society;
- gets tested for the coronavirus if there is any doubt of being positive, without the fear of being placed in quarantine.

This is really more a dream than a utopia.

William Shakespeare wrote, "We are such stuff as dreams are made of ..."

But leaving dreaming aside, we need to be able to capture and grasp the subtle and not so subtle signs of the traumatic repercussions of what has happened to us, not just as individuals, but as a society as a whole. We will need to attempt to heal a trauma like this through stories, personal accounts and recounting individual experiences. We will also need to deal with the various moods (guilt, denial, minimization, etc.) of those who survived, those who were not infected, and those who suffered no consequences. They too need help.

Our two diaries focus on the "psychoanalysis of the being and sensing", in the meaning of the Greek derivation of aesthetics from the verb *aisthanomai*, i.e., "perceiving through the mediation of the senses". We could call it "ontological psychoanalysis" as Ogden wrote in another context (2004). In an attempt to explain our definition better, an association came to mind from the cinema, which is a passion that we both share as a way of "sensing". We thought of Jean-Luc Godard's films and the stylistic and content revolution of this director's French new wave (*nouvelle vague*) cinema in particular. In one of the most important iconographic revolutions of the twentieth century, this director staged what was unthinkable before his time, starting with the film *Breathless* (*A bout de souffle*) in 1960. In this film he traverses several different genres, from colour to black and white, touching on different cultural references, from the American detective film to Groucho Marx. The French director shatters the imaginary wall that divides the screen from the stalls, giving the actors a chance to look into the camera in search of the audience's eyes. Godard summons audience members because he thinks they have a responsibility to take a position and serve as a witness: "The audience is responsible for what is projected in theatres", he wrote. And his wife would say that "in Godard's films it is more important *to be* than *to act*".

This is exactly what psychoanalysts were enlisted to "do" during the most dramatic period of the pandemic. They were asked to look after the being rather than merely interpreting or observing. This was a form of psychoanalysis in which the analyst is tasked with *being with a patient* rather than merely *being an onlooker* or *interpreter*.

What role should psychoanalysis play in this age of shared loss?

Just as art is often called upon to perform an ethical function – or perhaps even a political one since it forces observers to take a critical position – the experiences we related in this book lead us to believe that psychoanalysis should perhaps more deliberately reappropriate that very function. In our eyes, this is a poetic, political and social function, which we believe is eloquently depicted by the young African American poet Amanda Gorman, in her passionate reading of one of her "political" poems – *The Hill We Climb* – during President Joe Biden's inauguration ceremony.

Let us try to imagine that psychoanalysis is like this young, passionate poet.

Let us imagine, as was actually the case, that although we had to bear witness to White supremacists assaulting Capitol Hill, which was not unlike the mortal blow inflicted by Covid-19, we were also lifted up by the poetry and living poetic spirit of the poet. Psychoanalysis has been and continues to be alive and well with all its poetic passion, object constancy and dedication in the care and treatment of mental suffering.

We do not know whether "everything will be fine".

There will definitely be a lot to do and think about, and much to see and record.

This book is just one piece of our attempt to do our part.

Bibliography

Baldini, E. (2003). *Bambini, ragni e altri predatori*. Turin: Einaudi.

Barton, R. (1959). *Institutional Neurosis*. Bristol: Wright.

Bion, W.R. (1970). *Attention and Interpretation: A Scientific Approach to Insight in Psycho-Analysis and Groups*. London: Tavistock.

Bion, W.R. (1982). *The Long Week-end: 1897–1919*. Abingdon: The Fleetwood Press.

Bion, W.R. (2015). *War Memories. 1917–1919*. London: Karnak.

Bollas, C. (2018). *Meaning and Melancholia: Life in the Age of Bewilderment*. London: Routledge.

Bollas, C. (1987). *The Shadow of the Object: Psychoanalysis of the Untought Known*. London: Routledge.

Carroll, L. (1865). *Alice's Adventures in Wonderland*. London: MacMillan and Co.

Cassirer, E. (1984). *Filosofia delle forme simboliche*. Florence: La Nuova Italia.

Eliot, T.S. (1922). The Waste Land. In *The Criterion*, October 1922. New York: Horace Liverlight.

Freud, S. (1919). Das Unheimliche. In *Imago*, 5(5-6), 297-324. Leipzig; Wien: Hugo Heller & Co.

Freud, S. (1920). *Jenseits des Lutstprinzips*. Zurich; Leipzig; Wien: Internationaler Psychoanalytischer Verlag.

Kundera, M. (1984). *L'insoutenable légèreté de l'être*. [Nesnesitelná lehkost bytí] Paris: Folio.

Matheson, R. (1954). *I Am Legend*. New York: Gold Medal Books.

Melville, H. (1851). *Moby Dick*. London: R. Clay for Richard Bentley.

Montale, E. (1974). La solitudine. In *Quaderno di quattro anni* (1977). Milan: Mondadori.

Ogden, T.H. (2004). On holding and containing, being and dreaming. *International Journal of Psycho-Analysis*, 85(6), 1349-1364.

Petrella, F. (2018). *L'ascolto e l'ostacolo*. Milan: Jaca Books.

Pieraccioni, D. (1954). *Grammatica greca*. Florence: Sansoni.

Ricoeur, P. (1965). *De l'interprétation: Essai sur Sigmund Freud*. Paris: Le Seuil.

Rovatti, P.A. (2007). *Abitare la distanza: Per una pratica della filosofia*. Milan: Raffaello Cortina.

Sacks, O. (1984). *A Leg to Stand On*. Milan: Adelphi.

VanderMeer, J. (2014). *Southern Reach Trilogy*. New York: HarperCollins Publishers.

Verne, J. (1873). *Le Tour du monde en quatre-vingts jours*. Paris: Pierre-Jules Hetzel.

Verne, J. (1870). *Vingt mille lieues sous les mers*. Paris: Pierre-Jules Hetzel.

Woolf, V. (1927). *To the Lighthouse*. London: Hogarth Press.

Filmography

28 Days Later (United Kingdom, 2002). Director: Danny Boyle. Screenplay: Alex Garland. Production: British Film Council, DNA Films. Distribution: 20th Century Fox.

Alien (United Kingdom, USA, 1979). Director: Ridley Scott. Screenplay: Dan O'Bannon, Ronald Shusett. Production: Brandywine Productions, 20th Century Fox.

Apollo 13 (USA, 1995). Director: Ron Howard. Screenplay: William Broyles Jr., Al Reinert. Production: Brian Grazer.

Blade Runner (USA, Hong Kong, 1982). Director: Ridley Scott. Screenplay: Hampton Fancher, David Webb Peoples. Production: The Ladd Company, Shaw Brothers, Tandem Productions. Distribution: Warner Bros.

Bridges of Spies (USA, 2015). Director: Steven Spielberg. Screenplay: Matt Charman. Production: DreamWorks SKG. Distribution: 20th Century Fox.

Broadchurch (United Kingdom, 2013–2017). Creator: Chris Chibnall. Production: Kudos Film and Television. TV Original Prime from March 2013 to April 2017.

Cinderella (USA, 1950). Director: Wilfred Jackson, Hamilton Luske, Clyde Geronimi. Screenplay: Bill Peet, Ted Sears, Homer Brightman, Ken Anderson, Erma Penner, Winston Hibler, Harry Reeves, Joe Rinaldi. Production: Walt Disney Productions. Distribution: RKO Radio Pictures.

Cuori puri (Italy, 2017). Director: Roberto De Paolis. Screenplay: Roberto de Paolis, Luca Infascelli, Carlo Salsa, Greta Schicchitano. Production: Young Films, Rai Cinema by MiBACT. Distribution: Cinema s.r.l.

Dark (Germany, 2017). Director and Screenplay: Baran bo Odar. Production: Wiedemann & Berg Television. TV Prime: December 2017.

Finding Nemo (USA, 2003). Director: Andrew Stanton, Lee Unrick. Screenplay: Andrew Stanton, Bob Peterson, David Reynolds. Production: Walt Disney Pictures, Pixar Animations Studios. Distribution: Walt Disney Pictures.

L'isola sbagliata (Italy, 2019). Director and Screenplay: Giorgio Magarò.

La casa de papel (Spain, 2017). Creator: Álex Pina. Original TV Prime: May 2017.

98 Filmography

La pazza gioia (Italy, 2016). Director: Paolo Virzì. Screenplay: Francesca Archibugi, Paolo Virzì. Production: Marco Belardi. Distribution: 01 Distribution.

La stanza del figlio (Italy, France, 2001). Director: Nanni Moretti. Screenplay: Linda Ferri, Heidrun Schleef, Nanni Moretti. Produzione: Bac Films, Canal+, Rai Cinemafiction, Sacher Film, Telepiù. Distribution: Sacher Distribuzione.

Mary Poppins (USA, 1964). Director: Robert Stevenson. Subject: from novels by P. L. Travers. Screenplay: Bill Walsh, Don Da Gradi. Production: Walt Disney and Bill Walsh.

Memories of Murder (South Korea, 2003). Director: Bong Joon-ho. Screenplay: Bong Joon-ho, Kim Kwang-lim, Shim Sung-bo. Production: Sidus Pictures, CJ Entertainment. Distribution: Lucky Red, Academy Two.

Midsommar (USA, Sweden, 2019). Director: Ari Aster. Production: B-Reel Films, Square Peg. Distribution: Eagle Picture.

Modern Times (USA, 1936). Director and Screenplay: Charlie Chaplin.

Mother (South Korea, 2009). Director: Bong Joon-ho. Screenplay: Bong Joon-ho, Park Eun-kyo. Production: Magnolia Pictures. Distribution: PFA Films.

Nuovo Cinema Paradiso (Italy, France, 1988). Director and Screenplay: Giuseppe Tornatore. Production: Cristaldifilm, Films Ariane.

Oblivion (USA, 2013). Director: Joseph Kosinski. Screenplay: Joseph Kosinski, William Monahan, Karl Gajdusek, Michael Arndt. Production: Chernin Entertainment, Monolith Pictures. Distribution: Universal Picture.

Parasite (South Korea, 2019). Director: Bong Joon-ho. Screenplay: Bong Joon-ho, Han Ji-won. Production: Barunsun E&A. Distribution: Academy Two.

Peter Pan (USA, 1953). Director: Hamilton Luske, Clyde Geronimi, Wilfred Jackson, Jack Kinney. Based on the characters of J. M. Barrie. Screenplay: Ted Sears, Erdman Penner, Bill Peet, Winston Hibler, Joe Rinaldi, Milt Banta, Ralph Wrigth, William Cottrell. Production: Walt Disney Production. Distribution: RKO Radio Pictures.

Pinocchio (Italy, France, United Kingdom, 2019). Director: Matteo Garrone. Based on the characters of Carlo Collodi. Screenplay: Matteo Garrone, Massimo Ceccherini. Production: Archimede, Rai Cinema, Le Pacte, Recorded Picture Company. Distribution: 01 Distribution.

Pinocchio (USA, 1940). Director: Ben Sharpsteen, Hamilton Luske, Bill Roberts, Norman Ferguson, Jack Kinney. Wilfred Jackson, T. Hee. Based on the characters of Carlo Collodi. Screenplay: Ted Sears, Otto Englander, Webb Smith, William Cottrell, Joseph Sabo, Erdman Penner, Aurelius Battaglia, Bill Peet. Production: Walt Disney Production. Distribution: RKO Radio Pictures.

Sea Fever (Belgium, Ireland, United Kingdom, Sweden, USA, 2019). Director and Screenplay: Neasa Hardiman. Production: Bright Movie Pictures. Distribution: Eagle Film.

Snowpiercer (USA, South Korea, 2013). Director: Bong Joon-ho. Screenplay: Bong Joon-ho, Kelly Masterson. Production: Moho Films, SnowPiercer. Opus Pictures, Stillking Films, CJ Entertainment. Distribution: Koch Media.

Star Wars (USA, 1977). Director and Screenplay: George Lucas. Production: Gary Kurtz. Distribution: 20th Century Fox.

The Bay (USA, 2012). Director: Barry Levinson. Screenplay: Michael Wallach, Barry Levenson. Production: Hydraulx, Automatik Entertainment, Haunted Movies. Distribution: M2 Pictures.

The Day After (USA, 1983). Director: Nicholas Meyer. Screenplay: Edward Hume. Production: 20th Century Fox, ABC Motion Pictures. TV Original Prime: November 1983.

The Host (South Korea, 2006). Director: Bong Joon-ho. Screenplay: Bong Joon-ho, Won-jun Ha, Chulhyun Baek.

The Invisible Man (USA, Australia, 2020). Director and Screenplay: Leigh Whannell from the novel by H. G. Wells. Production: Blumhouse Productions, Goalpost Pictures, Nervous Tick. Distribution: Universal Pictures.

The Leftovers (USA, 2014–2017). Creators: Damon Lindelof, Tom Perrotta. Production: White Rabbit, Film 44, Warner Bros. Television. TV Original Prime: From June 2014 to Jun 2017.

The Little Mermaid (USA, 1989). Director: John Musker, Ron Clements. Production: Walt Disney Feature Animation, Silver Screen Partners IV. Distribution: Warner Bros Italia.

The Martian (USA, United Kingdom, 2015). Based on *The Martian* by Andy Weir. Director: Ridley Scott. Screenplay: Drew Goddard. Production: Scott Free Production, Kinberg Genre, TSG Entertainment. Distribution: 20th Century Fox.

The Witch (USA, Canada, United Kingdom, 2005). Director and Screenplay: Robert Eggers. Production: Daniel Bekerman, Lars Knudsen, Jodi Redmond, Rodrigo Teixeira, Jay Van Hoy. Distribution: Universal Picture.

Toy Story (USA, 1995). Director: John Lasseter. Screenplay: Joss Whedon, Andrew Stanton, Joel Cohen, Alec Sokolow. Production: Walt Disney Pictures, Pixar Animation Studios.

Trainspotting (United Kingdom, 1996). Director: Danny Boyle. Screenplay: John Hodge. Production: Channel Four Films, Figment Films, Noel Gay Motion Picture Company. Distribution: Medusa Film.

War of the Worlds (USA, 2005). Director: Steven Spielberg. Screenplay: Josh Friedman, David Koepp. Production: Amblin Entertainment, Cruise/Wagner Productions. Distribution: United International Pictures.

Index

Abitare la distanza 13
adolescents 3–4, 31, 39–40, 51, 54
"aesthetic paradigm" in psychoanalysis
  3, 11, 39, 48, 50, 57, 62, 70, 80, 95–6
age 11, 39, 48, 50, 57, 62, 70, 80, 95–6;
  developmental 39; vulnerable 72
Agenzia di Tutela della Salute 36
agoraphobia, induced 11
AIDS 5
air 57–8, 63–4, 67, 78, 83; fresh 9;
  high-pressure 78; open 9–10; thin 67;
  turbines 78
airports 64, 72–3
alarm clocks 31, 73
aliens 18, 37, 44, 62, 71, 80
alliance, with patients 63
"allostatic load" 14
alpha element 35
alpha function 35
ambulance 23, 48–9, 75–7, 87, 89; service
  74; sirens 6–7, 10, 22, 58; workers 75
American hospitals 69
anaesthesia 6
anaesthesiologists 1, 5–6
analysis 2–3, 10–11, 15, 18, 32–4, 49,
  54–5, 60, 63, 65, 71, 73, 90–1, 94–6;
  phone-based 2; remote 2; room 49
analysts 2, 12, 15, 19–20, 24, 39, 55, 95
analytic: devices 8; interactions 15;
  musicality 15; process 8, 19; relationships 44
anger 24, 92
anguish 4, 9, 20, 37, 50, 52, 66; absolute
  52; experienced when visiting positive
  patients 50; various gradients of 10
anti-decubitus pillow 51
anti-tubercular vaccines 50
antibiotics 74

antiviral drugs 5
antiviral medication 11
anxiety 20, 44, 46, 76; abandonment 37;
  primitive 52; unimaginable 21
anxiety-reducing medication 85
apartment buildings 13
aperitifs 26, 40
Apgar indexes 64
"Apollo 13" 25
artistic gymnastics 6
artists 18, 24
Asst *see* local health service facility
ATS" *see* Agenzia di Tutela della Salute

babies 10, 40
Bach 70
bacterial pneumonia 74–6
bacteriological warfare 75
Baldini, Eraldo 17
Barton, Russell 44
Battiato, Franco 21–2
The Bay 46
beach 37, 40, 46
beards 43, 80
Beatles 69
Beckett, Samuel 31
beds 5, 7, 11, 74, 79, 81, 83, 85
beers 23, 51–2
"Bella Ciao" 27–8
Bergamo 1, 6, 8, 10, 23, 69
beta elements 34–5, 50
"beta screen" 35
Bion, W.R. 5, 34–5, 39, 49, 60
Bionic concepts 34; *see also* beta
  elements
birth 41, 73
bisexuality 6
blackbirds 67

Index 101

blood 15, 19, 58; infection 76; samples 81; tests 54; washings 76
Bocconi, Andrea 69
body 8, 16–17, 19, 29, 36, 43, 48–9, 56, 60, 81; absent 19; declining 36; dislocated 19; person's 39; temperature 42, 65, 73
Bollas, C. 8, 34, 52
Bologna 56, 78
Bolognini, Stefano 2–4, 14
Bong Joon Ho 17
books 3, 13, 15, 18, 23–4, 27, 37–8, 46, 55–7, 91, 94–6; *Abitare la distanza* 13; *Children, Spiders and Other Predators* 17; *Disturbance* 70; *Institutional Neurosis* 44; *L'ascolto e l'ostacolo* 18; *On the Uncanny* 18, 24, 56; *Philosophy of Symbolic Forms* 32; *The Shadow of the Object* 52; "The Uncanny" (Freud) 24
borders 20, 24
Borgo Ticino 53
boyfriends 6, 9, 14, 29, 64
Boyle, Danny 23–4, 97, 99
bread 15, 58–9, 79
breathing 7, 35, 63, 80
Brescia 1, 10
breweries 52–3
The Bridge of Spies 86
brine 40, 58
bronchoscopies 50
bubble helmets 78, 82, 84
bureaucracy 75

C-PAP *see* "positive pressure mechanical ventilator"
call centres 7; organized by the Order of Psychologists of Lombardy 6; psycho-traumatology 7
calves 9, 43
"camp tent" 2–4
Campo San Lorenzo 27
canals 38, 41, 59
Canton Ticino 47
carbohydrates 51
care 6, 17, 39, 41, 70, 76–8, 80–1, 83–4, 88, 90, 94–5; better 80, 88; intensive 11, 82; loving 25; taking 11, 80
cases 10–11, 15, 50, 54, 86; clinical 15; first virus 1; positive 1, 6; rare 10; textbook 73
Cassirer, E. 32

centres 18, 21, 39; counselling 39, 51; emotional 21; internal 22; public mental health 39
Centro Milanese di Psicoanalisi "Cesare Musatti" 15–16, 18, 24, 63
cervical pain 48
chaos 32, 35, 51
"Chaos Theory" 33
Charlie Hebdo journalist 70
cheerleaders 83, 87
chest X-rays 7, 74
chickenpox 11, 21, 48
child neuropsychiatrists 39
children 6, 9, 15, 24, 26–7, 31, 39, 41, 44, 47–8, 58, 62; creative 31; disabled 67; frightened 52; guiding in the dark 9; health 31; small 13, 43
Children, Spiders and Other Predators 17
Chinese psychoanalysts 14
churches 10, 22
cinema 3, 17, 67, 94–5, 97
citizens 4, 22, 71, 73, 90
claustrophobic situations 29, 78
clean linens 82
clinical 2–4, 24, 27, 30, 68–9, 71, 73, 75–7, 79–81, 83–5, 87, 89, 91; contact 30; diaries 2–4, 68–9, 71, 73, 75, 77, 79, 81, 83, 85, 87, 89, 91; responsibilities 27; tests 80
clinics, crowded 54
closures 1, 30, 33; excessive 33; of markets 1
coconut milk 42
Codogno 72
Codogno hospital 1
coffee 29–30, 38, 40
Cold War 86
communities 2–3, 53, 64–5; centres for autistic patients in developmental age 39; Italian psychoanalytic 2; for minors 39; psychiatric 39; public mental health centres 39
Community for Juvenile Offenders 64–5
comorbidities 36
computer companies 28
computer scientists 22
computers 10, 22, 30, 53, 79, 81
concepts 14, 19, 33, 44, 51, 63; meta-psycho-logical 32; psychoanalytic 24; psychosocial 44
concerts 70

102 Index

conditions 33, 78, 89; clinical 76; health 84; human 13; new 15; respiratory 78, 89; social 75
confessional 10
conjunctivitis 21
connection 25, 51, 77, 79, 81; bad 48; human 77, 85; maintaining 78
consciousness 63, 66
contact 1, 4, 6–7, 9, 12, 15, 34, 36, 52, 54, 74, 76–7, 79, 81; barriers 29, 35; clinical 30; emotional 65; first 76; maintaining 77; making 71; physical tactile 39
control tests 90
convalescence 61, 70, 87
corneal herpes 11
corneal injuries 21
coronavirus 1–2, 6, 8, 21, 27, 36, 50, 61, 90, 94
corridors 16, 43, 64
Corso Cavour 23
Corso Indipendenza 35
Cortina, Raffaello 52
couch 8, 12, 15, 30–1, 39–40, 49, 51, 56–7, 61, 64; orange 16; virtual 13, 58
coughing 6–7, 70, 74
counselling centres 39, 51
countertransference 8, 33–4, 54
courts 47, 59
Covid-19 29–30, 38, 40, 78–9, 82–5; ambulance service 23, 48–9, 75–7, 87, 89; body temperature 42, 65, 73; danger 2, 31, 35; doctor patients 7, 10–11, 23, 30, 36, 43, 50, 60; health-care workers 1, 4, 20, 36, 38, 83; helmets 29–30, 38, 40, 78–9, 82–5; hospital wards 43; online sessions 6, 72, 91; pathologies 7; patients 1–2, 4–7, 9–25, 30–1, 36, 39–40, 43–50, 56, 59–61, 64–7, 70–2, 74–7, 81–2, 84–6, 88–91; pneumonia 21; psychoanalysis 2–3, 15, 18, 24, 32–4, 44, 46, 63, 71, 90–1, 94–6; and the sense of shame 76; Skype sessions 6, 9, 13–14; surviving patients 44; symptoms 1, 6, 8, 36, 54, 68, 71, 80; virus 1–8, 20–1, 23, 27–9, 31, 36, 44–5, 50, 52–3, 71, 74, 76, 88–90, 92, 94; young patients 13, 16–17, 19, 30, 56
CPS *see* Local Psychiatry Out-patient Clinic
criminal responsibility 5

crowded bars 23
crowded clinics 54
cultural references 95
Cuori Puri 32
"current neurosis" 36
curve, exponential 7, 75

danger 2, 31, 35
darkness 9–10, 12, 17, 56
The Day After 20
"day of liberation" 36
days 3–5, 7–9, 11–17, 19, 21–32, 35–50, 52–4, 56–67, 69, 73–6, 78, 82, 88–91; 1 5; 2 5; 3 6; 4 7; 5 7; 6 8; 7 8; 8 9; 9 9; 10 10; 11 11; 12 11; 13 12; 14 12; 15 13; 16 14; 17 14; 18 15; 19 16; 20 17; 21 18; 22 18; 23 19; 24 20; 25 20; 26 21; 27 22; 28 23; 29 24; 30 24; 31 25; 32 26; 33 26; 34 27; 35 28; 36 29; 37 29; 38 30; 39 30; 40 31; 41 32; 42 33; 43 34; 44 35; 45 36; 46 36; 47 37; 48 38; 49 38; 50 39; 51 40; 52 40; 53 41; 54 42; 55 43; 56 44; 57 44; 58 45; 59 45; 60 46; 61 46; 62 47; 63 48; 64 48; 65 49; 66 50; 67 51; 68 51; 69 52–3; 70 53; 71 54; 72 54; 73 55; 74 56; 75 56; 76 57; 77 57; 78 58; 79 59; 80 59; 81 60; 82 61; 83 61; 84 62; 85 62; 86 63; 87 64; 88 64; 89 65; 90 66; 91 66
"death drive" 34
"death knell" 69
deaths 1–2, 4–5, 24, 26, 34, 36, 69, 77
diary 3–4, 12, 23, 27, 32, 40, 55, 61, 66–7, 92; Angelo's 3; daily 19, 27; moving 42; old 66; psychoanalytical 2, 21
directors 17–18, 23–4, 51, 95
disease 48, 50, 68–9, 71, 73–7, 79, 81–3, 85–7, 89, 91–2, 94; associated 1; characteristics of 68; experience 3; respiratory 5
Disturbance 70
The Divine Comedy 65
doctor patients 7, 10–11, 23, 30, 36, 43, 50, 60
doctors 2, 4–10, 13–14, 19–20, 22–3, 25, 48, 50, 60, 68, 70–2, 75–8, 80, 83–5, 89–90; frontline 6; and healthcare workers 1, 4, 20, 36, 38, 83; sacrifices of 1; working in devastated wards converted into Covid-19 areas 4; young 75, 79
dogs 40, 44–5, 53–4, 67

Index   103

dreams 8, 10, 15, 17–19, 23–4, 30, 40–2, 59–60, 64, 66, 94; collective 24; variegated 29; young girl 59
drugs, antiviral 5

earphones 9, 14, 40, 56, 60
Ebola virus 5
emergency rooms 8, 68, 74–5
emotional experiences 34, 63
entropy 32–4; in physics 33; positive 34; rate 33; relative 34
epidemic 2, 10, 21, 23, 27, 52, 54–5, 61
experience 8, 10, 13, 16, 21–2, 34–5, 37, 47–9, 52, 54–5, 69, 82–3, 88, 90–5; alienating 52; catastrophic 2; of despair 66; disease 3; emotional 34; hallucinatory 53; hospital 70; individual 68, 94; intense 91; of joy and hope 77; learning 84; life-changing 84; metaphysical 35; mystic 53; prepandemic 73; reality 35; of the unconscious 55
experience, life 3
exponential curve 7, 75

Fatebenefratelli Hospital 76, 83, 87
Fatebenefratelli Institute, San Colombano al Lambro 18
Fatebenefratelli Psychiatric Hospital 45
fatigue 13, 73–4
fears 40, 52, 62, 66, 70–1, 73, 75, 77, 80, 87, 93–4; contiguous 31; experiencing 77; internal 88; sharing 61
fever 8–9, 14, 48, 73–4, 78, 80
FFP2 masks 6
Fiamminghi, Anna Maria 50, 53, 83
films 10, 15, 17, 20, 23, 25, 31–2, 42, 46, 54–5, 64, 66–7, 99; *28 Days Later* 23; *"Apollo 13"* 25; *The Bay* 46; *The Bridge of Spies* 86; catastrophic 20; *Cuori Puri* 32; *The Day After* 20; *The Host* 17; Italian 32; *La Pazza Gioia* 31–2; *Memoir of an Assassin* 17; *Mother* 17; *"Nuovo Cinema Paradiso"* 66; *Parasite* 17; science fiction 19, 29; *Sea Fever* 46; *Snowpiercer* 17; *Trainspotting* 23; *The War of the Worlds* 67
fingernails 80
Fontana decree 22
forearms 39–40
Frank, Anne 26
free associations 16, 19, 39, 44–5, 56, 66

Freud, Sigmund 8, 14, 24, 34, 58, 60–1, 66, 96
frontline doctors 6
fun pastimes 23, 41, 69, 75

gardeners 28
gardens 28, 41, 63
general practitioners 11, 14, 21, 25, 45; *see also* doctors
Giraud, Jean (known as Moebius) 17–18
glasses 7, 35, 40, 64, 83
gloves 5, 7, 26, 42–3
Goisis, Pietro Roberto 1– 4, 68–92, 93–5
GPs 45; *see also* doctors
grandparents 13
groups 15, 18, 30, 32, 46, 48, 50, 52, 65, 96; of brothers 50; clinical 30; research 24; small 62; social 54
gymnastics, artistic 6

headphones 79, 83
healing 77
health service facility 51
healthcare 1, 4, 25, 36, 38–9, 50, 60–1, 83; facilities 61; Italian 38; normal daily 50; workers 1, 4, 20, 36, 38, 83
helmets 78–9, 82–5
heroes 20, 88
herpes, corneal 11
herpetic pustules 48
heterosexuality 6
home care 74
homemade bread 15, 58
homes 7–8, 10, 13, 15, 20, 24–7, 31, 36, 41, 44–5, 48, 54–5, 74–5, 81–2, 89–90; containing hysterical mothers with children 9; earthquakes destroying 2; and hearing the audible ambulance sirens 6; of psychoanalysts 11; and quarantining due to contact with positive cases 6, 8; retirement 36
homework 53
homosexuality 6
hospitalization 7, 50, 54, 70, 75, 81, 83, 87–8, 91; advising against 8; difficult experience of 22; fear of immediate 75; and the influence of music during 69–70; initial 89; in a sub-intensive therapy ward for a very serious Covid-19 pneumonia 21
hospitals 1, 3–6, 8, 22, 25, 28, 38, 60, 68–9, 76, 80–1, 84, 86–90; American

104 Index

69; Bergamo 1, 6, 8, 10, 23, 69; Brescia 1, 10; Codogno hospital 1; Fatebenefratelli Hospital 76, 83, 87; Fatebenefratelli Psychiatric Hospital 45; intensive care units 7, 20, 68; Lombardy 1, 6, 11, 20, 36, 50–1, 65; Luigi Sacco Hospital 76; psychiatric 27, 39, 44; Sacco Hospital 80, 82–3, 87; and the Skype sessions 6
The Host 17
human beings 4, 20, 78, 83, 90
human bonds 39
humerus 39–40
hysterical nurses 5

I Am a Legend 19
images 9, 12, 18, 45, 49, 54, 63–4, 66–7, 86, 89; combative 18; first 89; forming 35
immune systems 11, 21
induced agoraphobia 11
infections 1, 73, 78, 80, 86
injuries, leg 48
Institutional Neurosis 44
intensive care units 7
International Psychoanalytical Association 2
intimacy 17, 27, 40
invisible aliens 44
invulnerability 72; *see also* omnipotence
IPA *see* International Psychoanalytical Association
irrigation canals 38
Italian films *see* films
Italian psychoanalytic community 2
Italian Psychoanalytic Society 2–3
Italy 7, 57, 69, 81–2; the first European country to be involved in the catastrophic experience 2; and the millions of people infected with COVID-19 68; and the mythical "Patient Zero", Mattia Maestri 1

Journal of Psychoanalysis 38
journalists 12, 70

Kundera, Milan 45

La Pazza Gioia 31–2
La Provincia Pavese 36
Lançon, Philippe 70

language 41, 54, 62; medieval Armenian 62; peasant 41
L'ascolto e l'ostacolo 18
latex gloves 42
lawyers 86
Lectura Dantis 65
leg injuries 48
linens, clean 82
Local Psychiatry Out-patient Clinic 54
lockdown 3–5, 7, 9, 11, 13, 15, 23–5, 31, 47–9, 51, 53–5, 57–61, 65, 89, 93; allostatic 51; heavy 45
Lombard Healthcare System 39, 50, 60
Lombard retirement homes 36
Lombardy 1, 6, 11, 20, 36, 50–1, 65
London 82, 88
long days 4–5, 14, 24, 30, 39, 46
love 14–15, 17, 21, 28, 40–3, 47, 62, 65, 84, 94; homemaking activities 11; songs 27
Luigi Sacco Hospital 76
lumbar vertebrae 9

Manara, Annalisa 1
masks 5–6, 21–3, 26, 35–8, 42–3, 45, 47, 49, 52, 56, 65, 73, 77; FFP2 6; FFP3 6
mechanical ventilators 7, 10
medication 11, 85: antiviral 11; anxiety-reducing 85
Memoir of an Assassin 17
mental work 12
metaphysical experiences 35
Milan 3, 6, 8–9, 15, 18, 23, 25–7, 30, 35, 46, 48, 89, 96
Milanese Centre of Psychoanalysis "Cesare Musatti" 15, 18
mind 6, 8–9, 12–13, 18, 29, 31–2, 40, 45–8, 51–2, 54, 63, 65–7, 69–70, 79–81, 86; healthy 73; open 84
mindfulness 81, 86
mobile phones 7–8, 10, 18, 24–5, 42, 45, 48–9, 61, 65, 81, 87–8, 90
Modena 9, 78
Momigliano, Luciana Nissim 16
Moretti, Nanni 26, 98
mornings 11, 13, 15, 19, 21, 27, 29–30, 35–7, 42, 45–6, 48, 73, 75–6
Moroni, Alessandro 7, 21, 24, 26, 28, 38, 46
Moroni, Antonio Angelo 1–67, 93–5
Mother 17
mothers 31, 39, 41, 43, 45, 56, 58, 83
movies *see* films

Mozart 70
Musatti, Cesare 15
muscles 16, 43, 51, 80
music 17–18, 27, 31, 38, 69–70, 79
mystic experiences 53

National Italian Psychoanalytic Society Congress 49
neighbourhood, working-class 59
neuropsychiatrists, child 39
newborn babies 10, 40
newspapers 11, 20–2, 29, 69, 91
notebooks 27–8
"Nuovo Cinema Paradiso" 66
nurseries 40, 64
nurses 2, 5–6, 22, 25, 36, 50, 76–8, 80, 83–5

offices 2, 4, 7, 9, 11, 15, 18–19, 59, 63, 66, 71–3
Ogden, Thomas 66
omnipotence 20, 28, 72
On the Uncanny 18, 24, 56
online sessions 6, 72, 91; *see also* Skype
oxygen 11, 55, 75, 78; saturation 89; systems 11

pain 1–2, 4, 16, 18, 23, 35–6, 39, 41, 46, 48, 64; and associated symptoms 71; cervical 48; life-changing experience of 84; suffering in vain 66
pandemic 4, 13, 32, 68–70, 79, 95; causing humanity to experience the unconscious 54; *see also* COVID-19
paralysis 46
Parasite 17
parents 26, 30–1, 39, 48, 55, 63; afraid of their children 31; distracting from 67; infecting 30
Paris 15, 19, 40, 96
patients 1–2, 4–7, 9–25, 30–1, 36, 39–40, 43–50, 56, 59–61, 64–7, 70–2, 74–7, 81–2, 84–6, 88–91; adolescent 7, 16, 24, 30; autistic 39; breathing 7; discharging 36; elderly 50; infected 77, 89; intubating 7; last 20, 29, 65, 67; positive 50; seeing 36; teenage 61; virus-positive 7; younger 13
Pavia 3, 18, 23, 26, 37, 41, 45, 50, 52, 59, 65
personal contacts 1, 27, 36–7, 39, 42, 44, 48–9, 55–6, 60–1, 63, 65–6, 69–70, 83,

85, 87; collective and personal mourning 18; contacting remotely 15, 36, 53, 67; facial gestures obscured by masks, glasses, headphones, screens, coats and other personal equipment 7, 83; using Skype 2, 4–9, 12, 14–15, 17, 19, 21–3, 25, 40, 44–5, 48–9, 60, 64–5, 67; using WhatsApp 2, 8, 14–15, 21, 36, 53, 71
Petrella, Fausto 18
Philosophy of Science 32
Philosophy of Symbolic Forms 32
phones 7–8, 10, 18, 24–5, 42, 45, 48, 61, 65, 81, 87–8, 90; *see also* mobile phones
physicians, primary care 1, 73–4
physics 32–3
pillows, anti-decubitus 51
pilots 33, 59, 64
plague-spreaders 76
pneumonia, bacterial 74–6
Po Valley 45
poems 8, 28, 47
"political" poems 95
"positive pressure mechanical ventilator" 10
possession 53, 59, 67; of physical and mental faculties 53; regaining 67
post-apocalyptic world 19
post-traumatic 22, 60, 91; pathology 91; sequelae 91; stress and disorder 22
practising "mindfulness" 81
pre-pandemic experience 73
preconsciousness 41, 56, 63
prescriptions 45
priests 10
primary care physicians 1, 73–4
problems 6, 15, 22, 25, 43, 48, 57, 73, 75–6, 78, 80–1; complex 32; heart 80; intestinal 74, 80; new 60; wrist 57
psyche 22, 35
psychiatric communities 39
psychiatric hospitals 27, 39, 44
psychiatrists 3, 6–7, 70, 85
psycho-traumatology call centre 7
psychoanalysis 2–3, 15, 18, 24, 32–4, 44, 46, 63, 71, 90, 94–6; "aesthetic paradigm" in 3, 11, 39, 48, 50, 57, 62, 70, 80, 95–6; effective 73; eliminating 90; ontological 94
psychoanalysts 2–4, 41–2, 68–71, 73, 75, 77, 79, 81, 83, 85, 87, 89–91, 95; Chinese 14; first 34; Italian 2

106 Index

Psychoanalytic Centre of Pavia 50
psychoanalytic community 2–3
psychoanalytic diary 2, 4–5, 7, 9, 11, 13, 15, 17, 19, 21, 23, 25, 27, 29, 33
Psychoanalytic Listening Group 45
"psychoanalytic phase" 57
psychoanalytic society 21
psychoanalytic techniques 34
psychologists 6, 9, 39, 69
psychotherapy 2, 51, 90

quarantine 4, 6, 15, 26, 52, 54, 57, 65, 89, 94; fatiguing 54; government-imposed 4

relationship issues 93
relatives 4, 6, 14–15, 20, 25, 31, 36, 39, 44, 48, 58; close 36; deceased 36; distant 48; young 15
remote 2–3, 13–15, 29, 35–7, 42, 44, 49, 53, 61, 67, 72; analysis 2; dialogue 3; meetings 36, 72; online platforms 2; supervision 2; teaching 53, 67
"repetition compulsion" 34
resistance 27–8
restaurants 59, 65
resuscitation 10
retirement homes 36
returning 44, 46, 55, 57, 59, 64, 66, 74, 79, 90; to being a patient 2; home 19, 89; to normal daily healthcare 48, 50
roommates 82, 87
rooms 4, 6, 8–10, 16, 21, 24–5, 64, 76–7, 79, 83, 85, 87; double 75; isolated 77; living 17, 25, 27, 55; new 50
Rovatti, Pier Aldo 13

Sacco Hospital 80, 82–3, 87
sacral area 57
sadness 9, 18, 37
school holidays 25
science 32, 94
science fiction 19, 29
Scott, Ridley 18
screen exposure (computer) 9, 40, 49, 83, 95
screenplays 17, 31, 41, 97–9
self-care 80–1, 90
seminars 56
sessions 5, 7–10, 12–15, 18–21, 23–4, 29–30, 36–7, 39–40, 44, 46, 49–50, 58–60, 70, 72, 90; first 61; focus on

new emotions 13; online 6, 72, 91; physical 91; Skype 5–6, 9, 13–14
The Shadow of the Object 52
sharing fears 61
short stories 19
Skype 2, 4–9, 12, 14–15, 17, 19, 21–3, 25, 40, 44–5, 48–9, 60, 64–5, 67; audio interference 16; meetings 26; sessions 5–6, 9, 13–14; video calls 8, 60
sleep 6, 13, 29, 34, 60, 74, 79, 85, 87
Snowpiercer 17
social networks 16, 61
society 33, 52, 94; adolescent 27; psychoanalytic 21
songs 22, 27–8, 31, 41, 69–70; love 27; old 35; singing Battisti's 17
space 12–13, 16, 37, 49, 55–6, 58, 64, 71, 78, 82; concrete 55; empty 59; habitable 56; living 13; mental 53, 67; new indoor/outdoor 30, 41; physical 4
SPI Coronavirus Emergency Team 45
Spielberg, Steven 67
stories 2–4, 7, 13, 16, 19, 39, 43, 54, 56, 68–9, 84–5, 90–2, 94; first-hand 69; mutual 87; short 19
studios 9, 13, 19, 24, 31, 44–6, 48–9, 55–6, 59–61, 64, 67
summer season 10, 25–6, 43, 46, 63
supermarkets 8–9, 11, 26, 42, 58, 60
supervision 2, 29, 48, 64; remote 2
supervisions, individual 48
surgery 5–6, 61, 70
survivors 18–19, 23, 69, 90
Swiss Neuropsychiatric Services 47
symptoms 1, 6, 8, 36, 54, 68, 71, 80
systems 11, 33–4, 50, 71; chaotic 33; expanding entropic 33; immune 11, 21; oxygen 11; peripheral vascular 43; physical 33; psychic 34; public health 74; therapy-oriented 90

takeaways 52
teachers 16, 53–4, 66
teaching 25, 53, 62, 67
teenagers 9, 18, 30, 49, 54–5, 65; living the "not yet time" 27; pre-psychotic 54; remaining hermetically sealed in their homes 55; talking about everything but Covid-19 6; young 72
temperature taking 26, 73, 83
"temporariness" (concept) 18–19
Ten Commandments 63

Index   107

tenderness 16–17, 36
tennis 16, 43, 51, 61
tennis courts 17, 47, 57, 59, 62
Third Analytic 67
time 2–3, 6, 8–9, 11–17, 19–20, 22–3,
 32–3, 41–5, 47–9, 53–60, 63–4, 71–2,
 75–7, 79–82, 88–91, 93; slippage 61;
 tested procedures 2
Trabucco, Luca 12
Trainspotting 23
transference (concept) 8, 15, 33, 39, 49, 60
trauma 2, 4, 22, 34, 36, 46, 60, 91, 94
truth 11, 19, 21, 23, 93
tuberculosis 50–1, 77
two-room apartments 13

"*The Uncanny*" (Freud) 24
unshaven beards 43
"unthought known" (concept) 51–2

vacations 25–6, 51, 65
vaccines, anti-tubercular 50
ventilators 5, 7, 10–11, 58
virus 1–8, 20–1, 23, 27–9, 31, 36, 44–5,
 50, 52–3, 71, 74, 76, 88–90, 92, 94;
 dangerous 1, 23; Ebola 5; novel 1;
 violent 4
Virzì, Paolo 32
voices 4, 14–15, 19–20, 43, 48–9, 54, 59,
 91–2; female 6; human 4; low 88

"war diary" 4

The War of the Worlds 67
wards 4–6, 17, 20, 22, 33–5, 38, 46–8,
 50, 52, 54, 60–3, 75, 77, 79, 82–3;
 clean 39; devastated 4; intensive
 care 20; speakers 6; sub-intensive care
 21, 68
water 26, 30, 38, 40–1, 54; blue 42; clear
 36; currents 30; gurgling 63; internal
 thermal 56; natural 51
Whitman, Walt 66
work 3–7, 9–11, 15, 20, 23–5, 33–4, 38–9,
 44, 46–7, 50–1, 60, 67, 70–4, 78–9,
 84–5, 90, 92; distribution of 90; hard
 65; mental 12; overtime 9; psychiatric
 18; psychological 71; theatrical 31
working-class neighbourhood 59
world 17–20, 26, 28–9, 32, 37, 40, 58–9,
 61, 67–8, 72, 77–9, 81–2, 84; fairer
 94; internal 35, 67; new 20; upside-
 down 68
World War I 24
World War II 4

X-rays 7, 74

young doctors 75, 79
young patients 13, 16–17, 19, 30, 56
YouTube 70

Zavattarello village 63
Zoom 2, 15–16, 20, 24, 48–9, 53, 55,
 64, 71

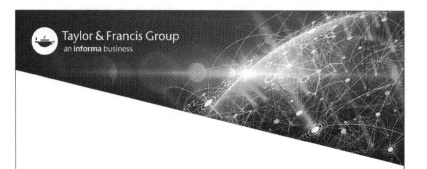

Printed in the United States
by Baker & Taylor Publisher Services